THE IMPOSSIBLE LONG RUN

My Journey to Becoming Ultra

by Janet Patkowa

Kindle Direct Publishing

ISBN 9781097716753

Edited by Gail Fay

Cover by BuzBooks

Excerpts of the Becoming Ultra Podcast were condensed and edited. Full podcasts can be found at www.becomingultra.com.

INTRODUCTION

The gun went off and I headed onto the course with the other runners. Morning was just starting to twinkle into the night sky, and a cool stillness prevailed next to the lake. The competitive atmosphere I had felt at every other race I'd started was not here. I was headed out for an adventure on the trails, and it didn't matter how long that was going to take. The race was fifty miles, and as Scott Jones, the creator of Becoming Ultra, told me, I had all day to do it. Becoming Ultra was a podcast show that followed the story of two runners as they trained for their first ultramarathon. They selected me to be one of the runners.

I was running in the American River 50 ultramarathon, just outside of Sacramento, California. As of six months earlier, the longest I'd ever run was a half marathon. After that half, I set my sights on a marathon. I'd been meaning to run one since I was a kid. So why was I on the Internet looking for something else to do? Wasn't 26.2 miles enough? My search was about something more than just running. I saw all sorts of adventures that I wanted to do, one day. The dreaded, evil one day. The phrase that lets you do nothing because one day is a fictitious date in the future when you will do everything you ever dreamed of, only that day never just arrives. I had to make one day happen, and dive into an impossible feat that forced me to take action. Something so impressive that one day I could look back and be proud of myself that I'd done it. I found the Becoming Ultra project. A fifty-mile adventure on trails! I didn't even know that was a thing. That was the perfect impossible thing for me to sink my teeth into and get me on an action path to one day.

However, that's not where my story begins. It's before that race, it's before I even decided to run the fifty miles. It begins in Las Vegas in 2014, two years prior to the ultramarathon. I was in a meeting with my employer when an event happened that made me reevaluate some truths about myself and reminded me that *one day* only happens when you get off your ass and start making it happen.

CHAPTER 1

I started a job in Henderson, the other city in the Las Vegas Valley, just a few years after the Great Recession began. So when the big wigs called an all employee meeting to discuss jobs and money, the mood in the conference hall was dismal.

I'd been through plenty of these types of meetings with my previous employer, and they always ended the same: "Just be thankful that you have a job." And I was, and I'm sure everyone else in the room was, too. Saying this just seemed like a cop-out for upper management so they didn't have to give us a raise. The only way I had gotten a raise in the past five years was to look for a new job and negotiate one. That's what moved me and my husband, Dan, from southwest Florida to the Las Vegas valley in the first place.

So, the big wigs started discussing upcoming changes and how they were looking to cut corners everywhere and how this would be affecting us, the employees. They said we could ask anything, that this was why they were here. I don't know what got into me because I don't normally like to draw attention to myself in situations like this, but I decided to ask a question. It just seemed that with all the proposed cuts and all the areas they said were already tapped, there was a gaping hole in their logic. I stood up and approached the microphone.

It was just like you see on TV—masses of people sitting in

a theater layout, an unmanned microphone in the aisle, and the department heads looking at you, waiting for the question. My heartbeat spiked in anticipation, sending waves of adrenaline through me. *Oh no, here it comes.* My voice does this weird thing when I'm nervous; it's obvious and awfully embarrassing. Like a speed-reader with a frog in my throat. I couldn't control it, but I had a question and I was gonna ask it.

"How are you going to make all these cuts without any of us losing our jobs?" My voice quivered.

"Oh, jobs will be lost," one of the big wigs said.

I heard gasping throughout the crowd of fellow employees. I wasn't sure yet if asking this was a good idea for my longevity or if I'd just put a target on my back.

My heart rate spiked even higher, racing faster than I had ever felt. My heart pounded from within and caused a pulsing lump in my throat. Adrenaline coursed violently through me, bringing wave after wave of intensity. My hands shook and I felt faint. I started sweating and my whole body throbbed. I backed up toward my seat and sat down while someone else took the mic and the attention.

CHAPTER 2

I leaned forward in my chair, my face propped in my hands, and stared at the swirling pattern of the industrial carpet. I didn't want my coworkers to notice that I was having a problem. I didn't know what was happening to me, and I wasn't prepared to deal with their reactions. I took slow, deliberate breaths and hoped for a calmness to arrive. Finally, my heart slowed to the point where I didn't feel it anymore, but my skin felt clammy and my palms were damp. I felt like I'd just run a marathon. Which was funny, because I'd never gotten around to doing that, so how would I know? I looked up to find the meeting was dispersing. My coworkers were standing up, so I joined them. I let them lead the way back to our lab; I kept to myself and didn't speak. Inside, I was filled with dread. *What the hell was that? A panic attack, or an anxiety attack? Was there a difference?* I had never felt anything so intense, something within my own body that I couldn't control. It scared the crap out of me.

"So, do you think we're safe?" one of my coworkers asked as we walked.

My hand went for an artery on my neck, and I felt my pulse; it was back near normal.

"Probably, but who knows," another replied.

My hand slid back down to my side. We arrived at the lab, and the group congregated to rehash the events of the meeting. I retreated to my desk and rehashed my own experience. This wasn't something that happened to me or my family. We have been blessed with good health. I was a runner, after all.

Well, I wasn't an actual runner at this moment. I thought of myself as a runner. When I was eight, my mom got me, my three brothers, and my sister into it. There was a summer track meet program at the high school that met once a week. We were all tall with long legs, so we had a natural knack for running. My summers after that were filled with race weekends across the state to compete in 10Ks. Then I ran through most of my school years on the track and cross-country teams. It was easy and I didn't have to try very hard to be good at it. I guess I thought you never lost that.

But there were signs that I wasn't good at running anymore. I was bartending in Florida in my twenties when a bar regular and I got to talking. He challenged me to a race out back. He was short and drunk, and in the past I could have beaten him easily. So, of course, I took the challenge, with a twenty-dollar bet attached. A group of us went out into the alley behind the place, and the two of us got set on an imaginary start line. I looked at my foot and thought of the hundreds if not thousands of start lines I'd placed my foot on. I could feel my inner runner being channeled. Another customer yelled, "Go!" I dashed off the line and my competition tripped in his first steps. *This is going to be easy*, I thought. I sprinted with every ounce of energy I could muster. The race was short, but he was quick. He recovered from his slow start and sprinted past me with ease. I was disappointed, paid my twenty bucks, and laughed it off, but I wondered what happened.

My adult life has had varying points when I really was a runner. I'd run a handful of 5Ks and a few turkey trots. However, since moving to Nevada, I settled into my forties with a life of ease. I went to work and then came home and told myself I deserved to relax. I'd watch TV and then go to bed. That's what adults with jobs do, right? I dabbled in exercise; I knew it was something important, but I didn't do enough and didn't do it with any consistency. I made pretty good food decisions, choosing chicken over beef and cooking at home instead of going out to restaurants, that was good, right? Of course that was during the week, the weekends were a free-for-all with junk food and fast food. And sugar remained a constant theme. So, maybe my health was not in balance. This heart episode was likely the manifestation of that imbalance.

I got up from my desk, went into my lab, and stood on the balance—the calibrated balance that I test every month for accuracy. That balance doesn't lie. I looked at the number: 161. My lips pursed—*161*?! I was twenty-five pounds over what I thought was right for me. I'm five foot nine, so I hid the extra pounds easily. But I didn't feel fine. For years, I'd gotten the sugar shakes, a term I'd been using to describe the shakes I got everyday around 9 a.m. if I didn't take in some sugar. For a long time I tried to blame it on coffee, but it happened whether I had caffeine or not. My hands couldn't rest still, and I had an all-over body feeling of anxiety that only a scoop out of the nearest candy bowl could calm. I knew it wasn't right, but I couldn't stop myself.

As I stood there staring at the digital number, I could feel the shakes coming on, so I did what anyone would do—I headed for my daily dose. And a few extra, 'cause it was just past the holidays and leftover chocolate Santas weren't gonna last forever.

I also wondered what I was going to do about all this. I needed to eat healthy and move more. But I'd tried that—in fact, I thought I was doing that, but something still felt off. A doctor could run a blood test and tell me what was really going on. I got a scare that day, and I didn't want to just ignore it. Maybe it was finally time to do something real about my sugar shakes, my excess weight, and my overall health.

I picked up the phone and made an appointment with my doctor.

The day of my doctor appointment arrived and I entered the waiting room. I took a seat and fumbled with my phone. A week earlier I had gone to get my blood drawn, so I was here to have the doctor go over the results with me. A woman in colorful cartoon character scrubs opened a door. My ears perked. She called, "Gertrude Paxton."

My anticipation was followed immediately by disappointment. Of course, it was too soon for it to be my turn.

A very large woman on the far side of the room struggled to get out of her chair. A much smaller man helped her, putting his arm under the woman's, but the struggle was all hers. I couldn't help but stare, even though I kept my head turned away. The humans of the world had gotten much larger since I was young, and it didn't look like any fun. I felt bad for Gertrude and wondered how this had happened.

Once my peripheral ensured Gertrude's back was to me, I turned my head toward her. She waddled to the door, the smaller man held it for her, and they walked through it, the door closing behind them. My gaze dropped to my belly. I didn't need to lift my shirt to know my gut was testing the stretch capabilities of my yoga pants, but in comparison, I was doing OK. I looked around the room and saw an elderly man holding a mask in his hand that was attached by a tube to an oxygen tank on wheels. Another woman sat with two children using their chairs as jungle gyms while a third nestled up to her wrapped in a blanket. I bit the inside of my lip. I shouldn't be here. These people are sick; they have real problems. I was just taking up precious time from an obviously overbooked doctor's office. I retreated to my phone and searched random topics on the Internet.

Several more times the cartoon-clad woman opened the door, called more names, and led people behind the door. Finally, she called out, "Janet Patkowa." I gathered up my things and proceeded through the door.

She led me to a chair and took my blood pressure. It was higher than normal for me, but still pretty low.

"Is that good?" I asked, looking for affirmation.

"Yep. Best I've seen today," she replied.

Again I thought, *What am I doing here?*

She directed me to get on the scale: 161. I already knew that.

"Is that bad?" I asked, searching for more affirmation.

"You're near the high end of normal," she replied.

A-ha! Normal indeed. I didn't like where I was, but I wasn't doing too bad.

She put me in an exam room and closed the door. Alone in the room, I looked at the jars and devices on the counter. I took in a whiff of a strong odor; the room smelled like every other doctor's office I'd ever been in and I didn't like it. I didn't want to be here. I thought back to my episode at the meeting. Was it really a thing? What could the doctor really tell from my blood? I needed to stay calm, not ask any more questions in rooms full of people, that's all. The door swung open.

My doctor walked in, swiping away at an iPad.

"How are you today?" she asked while continuing to swipe.

"I'm good; how are you?" The response was automatic. As if I was meeting a friend at a bar. That's probably not what she meant.

"What brings you here today?" She swiped away.

"Oh, just a checkup. You know. Haven't had one in a while," I said.

"Most of your numbers look pretty good. Any issues to discuss?" she asked. Still no eye contact.

"Oh well, not really. Well, I mean, there was this thing that happened at work. I'm not really worried, but I suppose I should mention it," I said.

She looked up, made eye contact, and listened as I relayed the story of my episode. When I was done, she said in a monotone, "Well, your sugar is high; that could explain your episode. If it remains high or gets worse, you're likely to risk diabetes. Let's get you on some pills to get that number down, monitor how that works, and we'll see you back in a few months." She closed the iPad and turned for the door.

My head tipped sideways, my brow scrunched as the corners of my mouth lifted. *Wait, what?* I thought. Then a little more effectively, I said aloud, "Wait, what?"

"Adult onset diabetes. It can occur in patients, like yourself, with high blood sugar. Don't worry; you aren't there yet, and there are many factors to consider. But with what you've described having happened to you, we need to get that blood sugar down, and with the proper medications you should be just fine." She looked at me with seeming sincerity, but with the kind of look I'd seen thousands of times working as a bartender, the look a drunk gets when he or she means well but won't remember you tomorrow. She handed me a sheet of paper with the prescription.

My eyes widened and my mouth hung open. Diabetes? Me? That was the most ridiculous thing I'd ever heard.

CHAPTER 3

When I got home, I set the prescription on the counter. I had so many more questions. Did my doctor state the cause of my episode? I couldn't remember what she said. Was it just high sugar? If I stopped eating sugar, could my number come down? How do you stop eating sugar? It's in everything! What were the other factors she mentioned? Was there something else I could do besides take pills? I should have asked more questions. The paper laid there with its bad news about me—*Me, are you serious? I'm from a healthy family. My grandfather almost lived to one humdred.* It was all about eating healthy and moving more, I knew that.

So, why was my sugar so out of whack? I knew how to be healthy. As a kid, my mom nurtured a full garden. We never kept junk food in the house. No cookies, pies, or candy. No chips, freezer appetizers like cheese sticks, or pop. (Yes, pop, not soda. I'm from the Midwest.) So I knew the basics of healthy eating. Sure, I indulged with a mini candy bar here and there, and two pieces of cake and ice cream every time someone had a birthday in the office. That's what adults do, right? And I wasn't only eating sugar, Dan and I even went vegetarian for almost a year. That was healthy, sort of. Cheese, bread, and pasta in excess isn't as bad as eating meat, right?

As for exercise, I was no Olympic athlete, but I moved around a lot. I even rode my bike to work; not many people do that. But I had to admit it was an easy three miles to work, and three downhill miles home. A few hundred calories burned. Not to mention that I couldn't remember the last time I'd actually ridden my bike to work; it was much more convenient to have my car when my lunch break was only thirty minutes. When I came home from work, I plopped myself down in front of the TV. A hard day at work, I told myself. I deserved it.

So how much was I really moving? Just carrying groceries up the stairs winded me. I told myself that it was the hot desert air, the higher altitude. In Florida, I was only about ten feet above sea level; here I was over two thousand. But I'd lived here a few years now; I should be used to that. So, maybe I wasn't moving as much as I thought I was.

I had a few errands to run and I had to get this prescription filled, so I went to change clothes. I took out a pair of jeans I hadn't worn in a while and pulled them up, but they were tight. I couldn't get them over my hips. I pulled at them and contorted myself like a circus act, but they just didn't budge. I layed down on the bed and maneuvered around until finally the jeans crested my hips and sat at my waist. I heaved a thick breath. *That was exhausting? Maybe there is something wrong with me.* I stood up and tried to button my jeans, but they weren't coming together. Determined, I took in a huge breath, struggled until I got them buttoned, and then let out all the air I'd sucked in. Ouch! Unidentifiable veins were pinched and pulsing at my hips. I went to the mirror and witnessed the muffin top of my belly spilling over the blue denim. It made me think of a banana nut muffin, and I wanted one. Those were healthy, right? With bananas in them? I went to the closet to find a shirt to wear. All wide bottomed. Suddenly I realized I'd unconsciously been allowing myself to expand and just trying to hide it.

The image I had of myself just wasn't accurate. I saw a person who was active and healthy and could do anything she put her mind to. But when was the last time I put my mind to anything? I wasn't fat by today's standards, which seems to be society's big indicator of being unhealthy. It didn't matter; I wasn't healthy. I don't like to feel like my body is all out of balance. I knew it wasn't going to get any better until I made it better. I released the tourniquet from my hips and changed back into my active wear.

I walked out of the bedroom and straight to the prescription. I picked up the paper and stared at it without allowing myself to read it. What I saw in front of me reminded me of TV commercials for prescription pills, when the voice-over comes on and speed-reads through a list side effects while a carefree skinny person rides a bike down a beautiful, tree-lined path. Filling this prescription meant going down the road of pill popping. Taking one medication, then another to counteract one side effect, and then another. I am not a pill taker; if there's a road without them, I'll take that. If I gave in here, the pill road would be easier, at least in theory. I'd have a doctor-sanctioned reason for not doing any work on this problem. But how much damage would I do to myself? Pills are hard on your liver, and they weren't going to solve my problem—they would only treat the symptoms. I needed to eat healthy and move more, not just in my mind but in reality.

Dan came home and I quickly folded the paper to hide the words.

"How was your doctor appointment?" he asked.

"Um, fine. I've got some errands to run," I said, changing the subject. I'm a firm believer that actions speak louder than words. I wasn't going to take these pills; I was going to take the road where I had to work at being healthier. I was no longer going to make excuses for myself. I tossed the paper in the trash.

"Need anything while I'm out?" I asked.

"Nope."

I walked out the door. When I got into my car, I sat and stared at the steering wheel. How was I going to get healthier? Running. That has always been my go-to answer. Whenever I feel like I need a health kick, I turn to running. But I'd done this before and it hadn't stuck yet, and after my heart episode, I couldn't chance a plan of failure. They say a sign of insanity is repeatedly doing the same thing, getting the same results, but doing it again anyway. So, I had to do something different this time. In the past, I would go out and run three miles. I should be able to do three miles, right? My inner kid shamed me for thinking of doing less, but three miles sounded really tough since my muscles weren't what they used to be. I could not go from couch potato to three miles in a day just because my brain told me I could. So, what could I do?

I decided that what I really needed was something to hold me accountable. At the time, the Fitbit was really popular; the ads were all over TV and the Internet. That's what I needed—a watch-like device that would track my steps and calculate all sorts of data for me. Like a pedometer on steroids. I turned on the car and headed to Best Buy. This was commercial advertising at work, and I didn't care. I needed a way to be accountable for moving more, and projects are way more fun when they start with new gear.

CHAPTER 4

Deep breaths, in, out, deep breaths. After getting home, I sat at my computer, held the Fitbit box, and stared at it. Contained within was what I needed—a way to track moving around. I went on the website and worked out my goal. I was at 161 pounds, and I wanted to get under 140. So I picked a goal of 25 pounds to lose. I needed to be moving around and burning about 500 more calories than I was eating. Walking five miles a day and eating 1,500 calories a day would work best for me. A sinking feeling plopped down to my stomach. How long did it take to walk five miles in a day? At twenty to thirty minutes per mile, that could take up to two and a half hours. How the heck was I gonna fit that all in? *Calm down*, I told myself. *All walking counts toward your daily five miles, so it includes walking to and from your car at work and stores, getting the mail, and taking the dog out.* I wondered how many miles I was already walking every day. I opened the box, took out the wristband, and tried it on. I read through the instructions and got the app set up on my phone. The app would track my movement, and I would enter the calories eaten. Calorie counting, yeah (deep sarcasm intended). There was no way around it. My mantra started at that moment: eat healthy, move more, eat healthy, move more. I'd make small changes, like park farther away from work and stores and take a short walk before work and on my lunch break.

Day one: I woke up about fifteen minutes early and walked around the parking lot of my apartment complex. It was dark and cold, but it was nice to get outside. I made one big loop and then went back inside. The Fitbit has a set of five indicator lights to tell you how you are progressing throughout the day. One light lit up after my trip around the complex, the other four remained dark. I rolled my eyes. This was gonna take forever.

At work I walked extra every chance I could. I had to; if I waited until I got home to fit it all in, there just wouldn't be enough time. I needed to get that indicator to three lights by noon. Every time I got up from my desk to go to the lab, I'd take a lap around the offices. I used a restroom in a neighboring building and then made a loop around the parking garage on my way back. By noon I had three lights. That was really encouraging. At lunch I quickly ate and then had twenty minutes to walk around. Yes, I just walked around the streets aimlessly. By midafternoon I was at four lights. When I got off work, I returned home and decided to take my dog for a walk. That was a disaster; she didn't want to go anywhere and kept pulling for us to go back inside. I guess she didn't get the memo that we were going to be active now. I picked her up and carried her until the fifth light glowed, then returned home.

After dinner, I got on the Fitbit app and entered all my food for the day. Yes, that part was a pain, but I didn't see a way around it. The only way I was going to shed twenty-five pounds was to get my eating calories and moving calories in balance. I didn't do too bad that first day; I even had about one hundred calories left. What better way to spend those than on a bowl of ice cream! If I had to pick one food as the only thing I would eat from now on, it would be chocolate ice cream. It's the perfect food: protein, carbs, and flavor! I looked at the nutrition information; I could have half a cup. I measured it out and put it in a bowl. No one likes measuring out a half cup of ice cream, no one. It looks so pathetically small, like putting an ice cube in the ocean. Apparently the calories in a bowl of ice cream in my couch potato days was about four times what it should be. I'd have to use a smaller bowl and spoon and just pretend it didn't look pathetic. I reminded myself this was not a forever thing, that one day I would enjoy a huge bowl again, but not today.

This is how it went for the next few weeks. I found that weekends were actually more difficult, because I was sitting on the couch more and I didn't have a lot of movement built in. The constant tracking was annoying, and I wondered how I was going to keep doing this. One thing that really helped: I stopped thinking that every change in my life was a forever thing. Twenty years from now, this Fitbit would not still be attached to my arm, surrounded by skin—a permanent part of my anatomy. I repeatedly told myself to slow down, to remember this was just temporary, a means to an end. I kept in mind that after a few months, I would remove this thing and move on with my life.

After about a month and a half, after steadily losing a few pounds a week, I was at 149 pounds. Twelve pounds lost! I was on a roll; my walks, eating, weighing—it was all working like a machine. Then, without any changes to my schedule, I stayed the same weight for a week. Then a second week. I started feeling really discouraged. I'd reached the dreaded plateau.

Anyone who has ever lost weight knows about the plateau. It's inevitable, but nonetheless it knocks down your resolve. I was putting in so much work. Walking extra anytime I had a spare moment to get that Fitbit to register another indicator light. Counting the calories in everything I ate. I was getting used to my half cup of ice cream and even learned to enjoy one small square of dark chocolate. How could all that no longer be working? I couldn't walk anymore; there just wasn't enough time. And I was hungry most of the time.

I turned on my computer and pulled up the Fitbit website. The data the device collected displayed the plateau in graph form. My head lowered. I told myself that this wasn't going to last forever. I just had to keep doing what I was doing and my weight would start dropping again. I was only halfway to my goal; I couldn't stop now. Being healthy never used to be so difficult. When I was younger, I ran all the time and ate whatever I wanted. Getting into my late twenties and early thirties, it was still pretty easy to keep my eating and exercising in balance. I was bartending then, so I moved a lot more than in my current sedentary job.

I looked back at the graph on the screen. I leaned in and tapped my chin with my index finger. Maybe there was something more I could do—more that I was willing to do. Calorie counting was starting to get annoying. I didn't mind measuring out rice and beans and cheese, but I wanted some snacks like chicken wings and a little bit of good-tasting bad food, like pizza. That wasn't going to get the plateau moving again. Then there was the walking, which was good, but I needed to incorporate something else. Running would be more effective, more calories burned in a shorter period of time. Yes, it was time to start running again. I'd been walking, and I was ready.

On the weekend, I got dressed in a big T-shirt, some shorts, and my sportiest pair of shoes. I put on an old Garmin watch that looked like a laptop on my wrist, went outside, and set out for a three-mile run. I'd done so many three-mile runs in my life, I thought this would be a breeze.

I set out at a good pace; it felt fast and I felt good. That's right, I was a runner! About a mile in, I was breathing heavy and hot, but I wasn't going to stop. By one and a half miles, I was exhausted. *This is ridiculous*, I thought, but I kept going. I looped around, and at mile two, I hit a hill that looked gently sloping, until I was halfway up and realized it had turned into a mountain. By the time I reached the top, what I was doing couldn't be called running; it was more like an agonized stumble. I was slouched over, holding a stitch in my gut. I continued to move forward. The last half mile took me forever. I'm too embarrassed to share the time.

I got home and felt a dash of accomplishment but mostly disappointment. When did this become so hard? The next day I could barely walk because my muscles were so blown out. I couldn't keep doing that; not only was it too much too soon, but I was going to lose my desire to get healthy all together. There had to be another way. I'd lost a lot of muscle from when I was younger. Being sedentary will do that. It snuck up on me, and I didn't realize how much was gone. I needed to go to the gym a few times a week. There was an indoor track at the local rec center with weight machines around it. I could do circuits —walk the track, stop at a machine and lift some weights, and then walk to another machine. Building up muscles while continuing to walk would help me burn more calories and get my plateau moving again.

I wondered if there was even more I could do to keep it interesting. I went on the Internet and found an app that peaked my interest. It's called Zombies, Run! It's like an audiobook: you listen to a story about a world overtaken by zombies. You and other survivors are in the safe zone, but you have the job of Runner. Specifically, Runner 5. The story describes your missions as Runner 5, and once in a while zombies catch up with you and you must go faster to avoid being eaten. This sounded like a great way to break up my walks and incorporate a little bit of running instead of three miles all at once. Plus, there were zombies!

With my new plan, I'd continue doing the Fitbit mileage tracking and calorie counting, but I'd add more intense exercises and thus burn more calories. This meant I could eat more and I'd also gain back some muscle. I started going to the gym twice a week and walked twelve laps (one mile), stopping at a different weight machine every lap. On the weekends, I went for a long walk and ran from zombies. I hoped that would get the plateau moving and get me down to my goal weight.

CHAPTER 5

I did it! In mid-May, just three months after I committed myself to losing twenty-five pounds, I weighed in at 136. I felt light and strong. My spirits were high, and I found it easier to have a positive attitude in general. I felt more like I fit into my skin instead of feeling hindered by it.

I continued registering five miles a day on the Fitbit, but that became much easier as my walks naturally started to include more running. I didn't force it, but my fitness level got much better and it felt right. My gym circuits felt slow as I looped the small track, and I could fit in more machines if I ran from one to another. I was deep into the Zombies, Run! story, helping the survivors get the food and supplies they needed. It didn't feel safe to walk out there with the zombies, so I started to jog and then run faster for the intervals when the zombies would see me. It was fun, and I felt great.

In the past, I had made exercise a struggle, something I must go at hard and get results quick, something that has to hurt. This time I wanted exercise to come more naturally so I could enjoy it as an activity that I wanted to continue doing. Having extra pounds didn't feel right to me, and if I could help it, I didn't want to be dealing with anymore heart episodes in my forties and beyond. I enjoyed the exercise I was doing and wanted to keep at it.

Embarking on a fitness goal takes personal commitment,

which isn't easy. There were times in those three months that my resolve was challenged. I hit a second plateau at 140 pounds, just shy of my goal. I just wanted to see that number dip below 140, but I had to wait for it. I had to continue to work for it. There were also days when I just didn't want to finish my goal for the day, when it had gotten too late in the day and I wanted to convince myself that I couldn't reach five miles. Some of those days I pushed the doubt aside; other days, I accepted that I wouldn't get there but didn't beat myself up over it. I woke up the next day and worked at that day's goal, and didn't try to make up for the previous one. Accepting my failures was part of learning to do this effectively and for the long term.

I learned a lot in those three months, and relearned things I'd forgotten. With food, I remembered just how many calories are in things and how much sugar is in everything. Portion size was another big one. Measuring out food isn't fun, and looking at the food on my plate with all the empty space was shocking at first. I learned to eat slowly and enjoy each bite. I learned to appreciate my meals and was better able to manage my hunger.

With exercise, I learned that I don't want to be lethargic about muscles ever again. It is much easier to maintain them than to try to rebuild them. As I get older, it's only going to get more difficult. I learned to pay attention to my body. I noticed a lower back pain when I bent over to pick up a dog toy, a sock, or to get something from a low cabinet. It was a pain I'd learned to live with because I just thought it was what happens when you got older. I was constantly aggravating my back and not thinking that those movements mattered. But I found that the stronger I made all my muscles and the more I paid attention to all the movements of my daily life, the less I had this pain. Increasing my muscles helped a lot and my back pain started subsiding.

I also learned that I had a long way to go. Losing weight was a great first step, an important goal for sure. But it left my face looking drawn and I certainly couldn't keep the portions so small over time, nor could I avoid foods I loved like pizza and chicken wings. I was going to have to figure out how I was going to maintain my health going into the future. How would I keep my weight down? What exercise would I continue to do? How would I balance that with the things that I enjoyed eating? I didn't have to make these decisions right away, though. I was proud of my accomplishment, and I was going to spend some time enjoying myself and not thinking about food and exercise all the time.

CHAPTER 6

My goal was complete, and I'd spent a few months with my mind on other things, running only when I felt like it. It was time to focus on a plan for maintaining my sub-140 weight. To do this, I wanted to run three times per week, but summer was in full swing and the temperatures were hot. In most climates, the day starts to cool off after midday. Not in the desert, where the heat continues to radiate and on the hottest days it can still be close to one hundred at midnight. To avoid the heat as much as possible, I got in two morning runs on the weekend but to get the third, I was going to have to run one day after work.

I changed clothes before leaving work and texted Dan, "Running from Lake Mead entrance, on the RMLT (River Mountain Loop Trail) out and back, about 5 miles total. Be home by 7." I filled my water bottle and headed for the park. As I drove east, the sun still high to the west behind me, I took a look at the temperature—ninety-eight degrees, a "cool" summer afternoon. This was too hot, but I had to get my miles in. I was keeping steady at my weight, and I didn't want to give up on my commitment to maintaining it. I pulled in to the barren parking lot, set my GPS watch, and started down the trail.

The first mile sucks, the first mile sucks, the first mile . . . always . . . sucks. I descended a twisting, turning paved trail down a hilly ridge. This trail loops thirty or more miles and skirts Lake

Mead for about ten of that. It's beautiful and desolate on a good day. It was desolate on this day because nobody in their right mind was out there. It was hot, like, surface-of-the-sun hot. However, after the first mile I felt good. So, I kept going, downhill toward the lake. Only a mile and a half until I would turn around.

As I ran, I thought about how far I'd come. I wanted to live life without health complications, and I was doing it. Running was great when I was a kid, and it was taking care of me as an adult. Easing into it by walking at first and then gradually letting the running evolve was a much better approach than brute-force running at the start. My weight loss goal was met, so now what?

I looked at the scenery in front of me—beautiful wide-open desert that gradually descended to the lake. Mountains lined the far shore. I was taking a photography class and learning about composition. I considered angles and elements that could make a great shot. I ran down further and neared the turnaround point. I was still feeling really good. It was hot for sure, but I had a lot of water left. I continued past the halfway, further downhill.

I had other things on my mind, too. Dan and I had been talking recently about all kinds of things for our future. The Internet can be a fascinating research source for the imagination. I saw people who lived in their RVs full time. They moved from campground to campground every few weeks. It sounded really interesting to explore the country with the freedom to move around in an RV. I couldn't do that now; I had to work, but one day, maybe when I retired. I also saw tiny houses. Really tiny, like, less than two hundred square feet. They were so cute and seemingly cheap to maintain. *Could Dan and I both live in one? Oooo look, a squirrel!* A small animal scurried across the path in front of me. *Oh wait, there aren't squirrels around here. Maybe it was a rabbit?* I looked ahead and the road continued to wind. I wanted to see what was around the next bend. I checked my water, and it was getting low. I decided to turn around.

The hill I'd come down looked completely different now. It was steep and glowing from the sun beating off of it. I started to run up. It wasn't long before my muscles were yelling at me. I was about three miles from my car. *One step at a time.* I tried to think about RVs, but my mind quickly shifted to the heat. I thought about tiny houses, and then the heat. I took a sip of water, but I needed more, and then my mind went back to the heat. One mile down, two to go.

Within the next mile, I drank the last sip of water. I was walking often, but it was hot, and there was just no relief. I felt light-headed but still able to concentrate. I continued, one step in front of the other. After making a sharp turn, I found some shade—a small sliver formed by the edge of a tall rock formation and the angle of the sun. I embraced it. I sat on the rubble at the base and let the cooler temp replenish me. And by cooler, I mean still awfully hot.

The car was now about a mile away. I didn't have a choice; I had to get back. The only question was how. And the bigger question was how was I going to keep up with my running schedule? Because of the heat, I really could only run twice a week, and I had to wake up super early on the weekends to do that. I could quit for the summer and pick it back up when the weather got better, but that was a scary thought. All the hard work I'd put in could so easily just evaporate, like the sweat from my forehead. *No, I am a runner, and a runner runs.* I took a deep breath of the less hot air in this shade patch, got up, and ran the last mile back to the car, slowly, so very slowly. I was committed to this, but I was going to have to be smarter.

CHAPTER 7

Throughout that summer, I resigned myself to running twice on the weekend. I couldn't run during the week without chancing heat stroke, and that wasn't worth it, right? Summer faded to fall, and I was barely adjusting to the milder temps when winter set in. It was cold and the days got short fast. Soon, the sun rose as I got to work and set before I left. In the summer, the heat made it difficult to keep running consistently, and now it was the dark. Maybe I'm too paranoid, but running alone in the dark makes me nervous, even if it's only 6 p.m. I was a runner, but technically, I was a weekend runner, and after my near-death experience in the desert during my six-mile run, I'd cut back to three- or four-mile runs. But what was six to eight miles a week really doing for me?

Dan and I decided to go home to Chicago for Christmas that year, so running got lost somewhere between planning, packing, and cookies. So many cookies—and candies and cheese spreads. As I stuffed some peppermint bark in my mouth and riffled through a selection of tree-shaped chocolates, I made the flight arrangements. We were headed to the great cold north. I rubbed my stomach, which had started to ache, and realized it was larger than it had been in a while. Runners don't have to worry about that; it was nothing. Sure, I wasn't running just now, but I was planning this trip and I didn't have time for it. I told myself I'd start running again after the New Year, once the weather got better.

A few weeks later Dan and I, with our dog, were in Chicago. There wasn't any snow that year and I was disappointed. Living in a warm climate, I enjoyed visiting snow and then leaving it behind. My brother-in-law picked us up at the airport and took us to his house, where his wife and their two boys were waiting. We began the week of holiday festivities with takeout from Portillo's, home of the best Italian beef sandwiches and Chicago-style hot dogs.

The next day, my mom came and picked me up so I could spend a few nights at my parents' house. On the way, my mom and I stopped to get a sack of White Castle hamburgers because how can you go to the Midwest and not have them? We got to the house and shared the burgers with my dad. Afterward, my mom brought out a tin of her secret-recipe fudge, the one she always made at Christmastime. This was the house I grew up in. The house I slept in after every race I had as a kid. I walked around the yard where I used to do sprints from one end to the other. It seemed much shorter now than it did when I was younger. Trips home are nostalgic because I don't get there very often; I wondered if it would feel the same to me if I could visit more. I also got to see my brother and his family. We shared a feast of turkey and mashed potatoes and homemade Christmas cookies.

A few days later, my brother-in-law and his wife had a Christmas party at their house and my husband's whole family stopped by. We feasted on lasagna and tons of pies. I enjoyed seeing everyone, discussing the previous year and what we planned for the next year. I hadn't put much thought to the future, so I came up empty-handed on that question—not many details to share. We enjoyed drinks and laughed, and once all the guests had left and our nephews were in bed, Dan and I watched National Lampoon's *Christmas Vacation* with his brother and wife, sharing lines from the movie before they were even said.

The next day, the boys were playing with their new toys and flying drones around the living room. My dog was huddled in a corner shaking like a leaf, so I decided to save her and take a walk. The colder weather seemed to entice her to walk without me carrying her. There was an extensive system of paved trails around the house, so I got in some distance easily. The path circled a lake lined with leafless trees and patches of reeds. The weather was mild, unusual for Chicago, and this looked like a great spot to take a run. I found myself with plenty of down time on this trip, and I could have run if I'd wanted to, but I hadn't brought my shoes or running clothes. Walking was fine with me; I just enjoyed the outdoors.

On the last night of our stay, we all went to Dave and Buster's—a huge arcade and restaurant that's a great place for kids and adults. My nephews ran around and showed us all of the games and how good they were at everything. They showed me car chases and shoot-outs. I laughed and that made them show me more. After each game, we collected tickets from the machines. We sat in the restaurant, had a Chicago-style pizza, and shared some obligatory smack talk about how it's so much better than New York pizza. When the night was done, we took the tickets to the shop to find out what we could get. As my nephews and their parents worked on turning those tickets into credits, I walked around looking at the gifts. In the corner was a giant scale with a dial and pointer. I hadn't been on a scale in a while. I looked at myself and thought I was doing pretty good. Sure, I hadn't run in a few weeks—or was it more than a month? When was the last time I'd run? I stepped on the scale, and the pointer swung far. When it settled, it read 146. I'd gained back ten pounds.

This is not happening! I'd put in so much work to get from 161 to 136, and I wasn't going to let that slip away. I got back from our Christmas trip on a Friday, and on Saturday, I took my running shoes out from the closet and sat down in the living room to lace them up. I caught a glimpse of my suitcase in the corner of the room. *I should get the laundry started before I go.* I left the shoes next to the couch and opened the suitcase. I collected items that weren't getting washed and put those away. I returned for my clothes and took them to the laundry room.

As I loaded the washing machine, my phone rang. I picked it up—my mom was calling. I winced. I'd forgotten to call her to say that we'd made it back safely. I had to take this call.

"Hi, Mom," I said after securing the headphones and slipping my phone in a pocket. Calls with my mom were too long to hold a device to my head the whole time.

We chatted about the trip, we chatted about the weather, and we chatted about current events. I might as well get something done while we talked, so I started cleaning the apartment.

Close to an hour later, we ended our call. The laundry was well underway and the place was close to fully cleaned. I got out the vacuum cleaner to finish the job. When I got to the living room, I picked up my running shoes. I let out a deep breath and widened my eyes. I could have been done with a run by now, but at least I was getting stuff done.

The front door swung open, and Dan came in.

"I would have helped you," he said gesturing at the vacuum.

"I was talking to my mom," I replied. We gave each other a knowing glance.

"Got it. When you're done, you wanna hit the grocery store?" He asked, taking off his sweatshirt and hanging it in a closet.

I looked at the shoes now under a chair and bit my lip. "Uh, yeah, sure."

Grocery shopping had to get done, right? We'd been gone over a week and the fridge was empty. After compiling a list, we headed out the door. The air was brisk and cut right through me. I hunched up my shoulders. *Do I want to run when it's this cold out?* When I was younger, I ran when it was raining, snowy, and icy. *Do I need it to be perfect weather to run?* This was a pretty sad thought, because comparatively, my weather wasn't bad. I never had snow to deal with, and half the country currently sat under a blanket of the stuff. What was I going to do? I could start a gym regimen, but I didn't like the gym. I loved being outdoors. I wondered when it had become too uncomfortable to enjoy.

After a short drive, we got to the store. Our teamwork skills at the grocery store are nothing less than amazing. I manage the list, while Dan wields the cart. I read off short segments of the list for him, then I went and got other items. We were swift and calculated. I thought about how quick we were moving and reasoned that there'd be plenty of time to run when I got home. In under an hour, we were back home and had everything put away.

I plopped down on the couch and Dan turned on the TV. I saw my shoes still under the chair. *Dang it. I was gonna run.* I sat up while Dan pulled up the DVR list. "Wanna get one of these out of the way?" he asked.

I squinted and curled the corner of my lip up. "I guess?" I laid back down.

He selected a program. It was an hour long; I could run when it was over. Except when the program ended, it was dark outside. *Dang it!* I had forgotten how short the days were. *I can't run now. How did the day get away from me?* I picked up my computer and googled "winter workouts." The results showed gym routines and living room workouts. I had to keep running. The heat in the summer and the dark in the winter were never going away; how was I going to fit it in? How was I going to stay motivated? My mind was all over the place. I needed something to keep me on track. I needed to pick out a goal. Something to work toward and focus on. Maybe I should try a half marathon. I'd only done one in my younger running days. I searched Google for races near me. I found a site called Desert Dash that listed trail races. I loved cross-country as a kid, so maybe I should try one of those. They had a race in May called Trails of Fury, a half marathon on desert trails. That was it, that's what I needed—a race to train for. I was going to run in the Trails of Fury.

CHAPTER 8

Over the next few months, I put myself on a doable training plan. I found the Hal Higdon website and adapted one of his half marathon training plans. I ran once during the week. It was dark after work, so I found a populated park with a lit mile loop and I did three miles. Once per week I did strength training at the gym. On the weekend, I ran my long run on Saturday, and then I ran a second time on Sunday for about four miles. In total, I was getting up to eighteen miles a week. I hadn't signed up for the half marathon yet; the website showed "Coming Soon" when I clicked the registration button.

On one of my long run days at the beginning of May, I got up and ate a small portion of oatmeal and a banana. I poured myself a cup of coffee, grabbed a sheet of paper, and moved into the living room, where I drew out a map for Dan to show him my route. I sat back on the couch, held my mug with both hands, and looked at the loop. A smile inched up my face. I was going to make a loop around town that I'd only driven before. I was going to run eleven miles: across a bridge that was two miles away, through the dog park that was five miles away, back through downtown and past my work that was three miles away. Butterflies fluttered in my stomach. *Can I make it that far?* I wondered. *How cool will it be when I finish and know I can do it?!* I took a sip.

I got up and put the map on the kitchen counter, and then went to the closet to get dressed. After donning my running outfit, I headed out the door. The first few miles passed easily and slowly. It was early and there wasn't much traffic. I passed house after house; I wondered if the occupants were awake having coffee. Several newspapers in the street indicated people were still sleeping. Not me; I was running.

I observed landscaping elements both good and bad. I liked the tiny path weaving through one front yard but didn't like the overly cluttered flower pot garden in another. If I ever owned a house again, I might put a path in. Dan and I got out of our house in 2011, after the housing disaster, and we were lucky to have broken even. We were in no rush to pick up another mortgage.

After about five miles, I was still feeling good. I thought about how far I was from home. *Impressive!* I gave myself a mental pat on the back. I navigated some paved trails that passed a casino. My senses heightened. It was early, so anyone in the parking lot now was likely to have been out all night. Having worked in bars for a decade, I knew the toxic mix of alcohol and the early morning light. It was best to steer clear of anyone I might run into. I saw one person hanging out by the dumpster. I stayed on the path and kept him in my peripheral; I got past him without incident.

Around mile nine I passed through a park; the bike path that led back home was on the far side. To get there, I had to climb a pretty big hill. I'd run the whole way so far, but this hill was huge. I ran slowly and climbed some stairs in the playground to bypass some of it. I made it to the top and started down the bike path. Over the next mile, I could no longer deny the problem that had been brewing over the past few weeks as the miles climbed: my left knee ached with every step, to the point that I dreaded hitting the ground with my left foot. The pain wasn't intense, but it was dull and increased the farther I went. No pain, no gain, right? I wasn't so sure. That's something a high school coach can say to a bunch of teenagers with bodies that can handle tons of stress. I was in my early forties; was I hurting myself? About ten years earlier, that knee had been giving me pain so I had an arthroscopic procedure done. The doctor removed some extra tissue from the meniscus area. Was running something I should be doing after that? By the time I finished, my knee was yelling at me to stop. I reached my mileage goal about five hundred yards from home and hobbled to the house. That was only eleven miles; I wondered how I was I going to run thirteen. And the trail was going to be steep. Would my knee break?

At home I got off my feet and did some stretches. Overall, I felt good about the run—I felt refreshed by the miles. But my knee throbbed. After a hot shower, I got comfy on the couch and positioned an ice pack on my knee. I wanted to do this trail half; there was no way I was going to let this knee problem be the reason I didn't run it. I wanted to know that I could put my mind to this goal and succeed. I knew if I signed up for the race I'd be committed to it and wouldn't back out, but the last time I had checked the registration still wasn't open. I reached for my laptop that was on the coffee table next to me, and pulled up the website. The Trails of Fury half marathon had a big red slash through it. The race was cancelled.

CHAPTER 9

Cancelled? You've got to be kidding me! That race was perfect for me. It landed on the weekend when I'd be most prepared, it was a challenging course in a trail system I hadn't seen, and it was early enough in the summer that the weather wasn't going to be super-hot yet. The cancellation ruined all of my hard work! I adjusted the ice pack still resting on my knee and searched the web page for an explanation. The course was in an area that needed certain permits and those couldn't be acquired. So, no race.

I rubbed my forehead with my hand and stared at the computer screen. What was I going to do? I wanted to have a race to complete so that I could set it in my head that I could accomplish something I put my mind to. I searched the Internet for other races. I came across two and rolled my eyes. I'd already been through all of the reasons why these two races wouldn't work. One was the next weekend, way too soon since I was only up to eleven miles. The other was two weeks after the race I wanted to sign up for—too far into the summer. Las Vegas doesn't kid around when the summer kicks in. It could easily be a high of one hundred on that day. This half marathon was going to be challenging enough for me; I didn't need heat to be an added factor. These weren't going to work. So what, no race? I was going to have to run for running's sake? I felt water dripping down my leg from the ice pack. I wiped my leg with a towel and put the pack back in the freezer.

I took the Hal Higdon training plan off the fridge and looked at all the cross-outs—runs I'd done in preparation for the half. I nodded my head in approval of what I'd accomplished. This was good, regardless of whether there was a race. I looked down at my frozen knee and wondered how far I could have gone anyway. Maybe I wouldn't have even finished the race. Was any of this worth hurting myself? Maybe the race being cancelled was a sign that increasing miles was not good for me.

However, I felt strong in other ways. Since getting some control over my body's food-fitness balance, I felt like I had a say in my future well-being. I wanted to do my part in my own health so that if the doctor one day said to me, "You have ailment X," that X would be something I couldn't have done anything to prevent. I never wanted to hear, "You have ailment Y, but based on the fact that you eat three pounds of sugar every day and live a sedentary life, I'm not surprised." I had control over that food-fitness aspect of myself, and I wanted to maintain that control. A race wasn't necessary to do that. But how well could I keep myself accountable? That was the whole point of picking out a race in the first place. I'd gained back ten pounds before Christmas thinking that I could just stay on track by sheer will.

No, I needed a goal; I work better with a goal. I decided to pick one of those other races. If I couldn't finish it, so be it. I couldn't do the one in a week, it was just too soon, so I chose the other one: the Wildlands Fire Awareness Half to benefit firefighters who work to protect our natural land areas from fire. It was in a beautiful park on the west end of the valley, Red Rock Canyon National Conservation Area. Now I had a few extra weeks to prepare for it, and I hoped the heat stayed at bay.

I woke up the morning of the half marathon and took in a quick breath. This was it—this was the day I'd trained for. I reached for my phone from the bedside table and pulled up the weather report. High of 101. My eyes widened. This was worst-case scenario for me; I recalled my near-death experience out in the desert, me hiding in a sliver of shade. How stupid was this idea? I wasn't going to drop out without trying, so I put down the phone and got up.

When I arrived at the start line, the temp was already close to eighty degrees. The race director gave a short speech and warned everyone to be aware of the heat and the effect it could have on you. I looked at my hand-held water bottle and wondered if it would be enough. I drink a lot of water and feel the effects of dehydration quickly. I decided to carry a second water bottle and went to a cooler the race director had supplied to grab another one. Shortly, the race started and I headed out on my first trail half marathon.

The first mile progressed slowly; I had to maneuver around people, and the course was uphill. There was a slight reprieve for mile two when the course went downhill, but the following few miles just kept going up. I had no choice but to walk a lot of it. I ran out of water in my bottle. I was glad I grabbed that second one and broke into it.

The scenery was gorgeous. I'd been in the Red Rock Conservation Area before but I'd mostly just driven around. Now I was deep in the park and seeing it from the trail like I'd never seen it before. I ran to a section with numerous large, flat sandstones that were in the way of the trail. I climbed on top of the rocks, and saw the trail start up again on the other side. The other runners were doing the same thing, so I assumed that we were still on course. I felt like a kid, again, getting to play around, climbing and jumping over the rocks. I didn't care that I was walking a lot of it; this was amazing. The sun hadn't crested all of the mountains yet, so there was a lot of shade and it felt relatively cool.

I then got into some single-track trail that was exposed to the sun and it started to feel hot. I approached a girl ahead of me and needed to pass her. She was wearing headphones, so all of my verbal attempts at warning her went unheeded. I tried several times to find an open section to pass her, but the trail was narrow and the cacti along it were bristly. I had no choice but to tap her on the shoulder, which scared the crap out of her. I passed her and moved on. I don't like using headphones on the trail. I want to enjoy the peace and serenity around me.

As I entered an aid station, I heard the race staff discussing a man who passed out somewhere. This heat was no joke, and I took it seriously. I looked at their supplies. I grabbed some Gatorade and drank it, refilled my handheld water, and grabbed another bottle. I got back to running. When I made the turn for the final stretch, I had about three miles left. This was a straight shot back through the middle of the park and a barren stretch of desert. I could see the whole park at that point, and I looked around at the stretch of red rocks to the north that I'd just run/walked through. It was so far away. I felt an overwhelming sense of pride that I'd just come from there. I traced with my eyes the course I'd followed and was impressed that I was still moving. This was a distance I had only gone in a car before. Not today!

Those last three miles were tough. It was hot and I was tired. I was going with only the power of my legs and mind. Thankfully the trail was downhill. My knee throbbed and I cringed at the pain with each step, but I dug deep and just took it one step at a time.

I finished. In three hours, but I finished. My goal was complete. As I stared at the finish line and looked around at the park (that I just owned!), I thought, *What next?*

CHAPTER 10

Later in the day, after the half marathon, I met a friend on the Las Vegas strip; she was in town on a work trip. Living in Las Vegas means that a lot of people visit for various reasons, so it's pretty easy to see friends who live far away. After having some lunch, we decided to go the MGM and tour the CSI Experience since we both work in forensics. My knee hurt and my muscles ached, but I tried to walk as normally as possible. I knew I probably wouldn't be able to move tomorrow, but I could make it work today.

The Las Vegas strip involves a lot more walking than people realize. The buildings look close together because they are huge and give a false sense of perspective. Leaving one casino to visit another that's right next door could involve a half mile or more of walking. *Haven't I gone far enough today?* I laughed to myself.

As I walked through the crowds and looked at the people around me, I wondered how many of them had run a half marathon today—or at all. I smiled. I was proud of what I'd done, and thinking it was not something many people accomplish made me walk a little taller. After the CSI Experience, we headed back to the Paris hotel. More walking.

We took the elevator to the top of the Eiffel Tower to visit the sky deck. When we got there, I realized my friend was deathly afraid of heights.

"Why did you come up here?" I asked. I lived in town; I could come here whenever I want. Did she do it because she thought I wanted to? Or to see if she wasn't as afraid as she thought? I never got a straight answer because she was shivering and holding on to a center pole. I decided to take a quick look around so we could get back down to the ground.

I stepped away from the center and looked over the edge. It was nighttime and the strip was lit up; with the gentle, warm breeze wafting by, the scene was so serene. We were over 500 feet in the air. *My trail race took me over 1,500 feet of elevation gain,* I thought. *That's three times this high!* I looked out past the lights to the west end of the valley where the race had been and thought about how good I felt having completed it. I couldn't stop smiling with pride. Then the postrace question recurred to me: what next?

A new goal did not immediately come to me, but I had another problem to contend with: summer was here. After-work temperatures were getting too hot for running. I had to find a new way to get miles in. I couldn't take multi-month breaks and expect to be where I wanted. Where exactly was that? I wanted to be healthy and running offered that. As long as I ran consistently about three times per week, I didn't have to worry about calories that much. It was easier to keep my hands out of the candy bowls at work so my 9 a.m. sugar shakes were subsiding. Being healthier made it easier to eat better most of the time, and not stress about an occasional splurge. So, no more denying a piece of cake at an office birthday party or saying no to pizza on a Friday night.

Mornings were my only hope. The temperature would be the coolest then, but it was dark at that time. I loved the trails, but I couldn't head out on dark trails alone. If I wasn't alone, then I could, but that meant finding someone to run with. The thought wiped the smile from my face. I hadn't run with anyone since high school, and the thought of it made me anxious. I looked down at the Bellagio fountains dancing to music and let my mind relax. I would worry about running with people another day.

That day came a week later. After seven days of hobbling around like an old lady while my knee recovered, I was finally ready to run again and to address the question of what next. I sat on my couch and opened my laptop. I needed to get on a consistent schedule. Summer was just beginning, and I didn't want a repeat of last year when I gave up running because it was too hot. I typed "running groups near me" in the search bar.

Several groups popped up: a running group in Meetup.com called Wild Bunch, a Facebook group called Run Grrrls Run, and Desert Dash, the local race company that had cancelled the Trails of Fury race; all three held group trail runs. I took my hands from the keyboard and folded them, interlacing my fingers, digging one thumb deep into my opposite palm. I considered what a running group might be like. There would be meeting times, but I liked to run when I wanted to. I didn't want to plan; I wanted to grab my shoes when I was ready and go out the door. *I just want to run*, I thought. There would be meeting people, and I'd have to try to remember names and faces. I don't remember people until I've met them a few times, so if I see someone before their face is imprinted in my brain, I can't remember them. It's been embarrassing at times when I've had a long conversation with someone and then the next time I see them, my mind is just blank and I have to try to remember why this person is talking to me. *I just want to run.* There would be talking while running. I'd seen pairs of people out on my runs holding a conversation and I thought how free was I to just do my own thing. I often saw two women running together and assumed it had to be two moms gabbing about children. I don't have children; would I have to listen to mom advice? And what if there were guys involved in these groups. They would be way too fast for me and I'd just be a hindrance. *I just want to run!*

There had to be another way. I put my hands back on the keyboard and typed, "Running when it's too hot." A picture of my worst nightmare appeared: a treadmill. I slammed the laptop shut. That wasn't going to happen. I loved being outdoors, and there was no way the answer to running in the summer was a treadmill. I'd rather eat pints of ice cream while I slowly blended into my couch than take up treadmill running. I was going to have to join a running group. I could at least try it, right? I reopened my laptop and looked at the running group results.

I liked the Desert Dash group. They ran on the trails in the valley and I loved being out on the trails. One of their group runs was early on Wednesday mornings and met at the McCullough Hills trailhead just a few minutes from me. On Facebook, they had an event and I clicked the "Going" button. It was official. I was going to meet a running group.

Then it hit me: what if these people were psychos? I didn't know any of them and I was meeting a bunch of strangers to go run in the dark in the desert? That didn't sound even remotely safe. My breathing started elevating and I had to stop, calm down, and think about this logically. If I were a murderer, this would be a bad plan. Who posts on Facebook to get a bunch of people together to run, only to kill one or more of them? Seems like there'd be too many witnesses. Plus, if someone was murdering people out in the desert, I would have heard about a bunch of missing people by now. This was ridiculous; I shut my laptop and put these thoughts out of my mind.

A few days later, I woke up early and headed to the trailhead. A handful of people were waiting in running gear. I walked up, recognized the organizer Kaylee from the Facebook page, and introduced myself. Then came the awkward standing around in a group of people I didn't know just hoping the small talk wouldn't start. Kaylee asked everyone what they planned to run. The route was a four-mile loop with a half mile out and back at the far end to make it a five-mile run. I wasn't feeling confident about that and I didn't want to hold anyone up, so I told them I was going to just do the four-mile loop. Kaylee looked at her watch, noted that everyone she expected to be there was there, and we started down the trail promptly at 5 a.m. I liked that; no wasting anyone's time. A few people grouped together and chatted, but I let them drift away from me and I ran on my own.

To the east, light was creeping up from behind the mountains, just beginning to light up the dark sky. There was enough light to see without having to use a headlamp. It was peaceful and freeing to be out there so early. Once I got down the trail a few miles, I had a view of the sun as it rose, drowning out the lights from town as they twinkled in the last shadows of darkness. It was breathtaking. We all got back to the trailhead and waited for the last person to arrive. I said good-bye to everyone and left. I wasn't murdered, I wasn't forced into an awful social situation, and I felt more energized than if I had consumed a whole pot of coffee. I left with a huge smile on my face and the confidence that I would make it through the summer as a runner.

CHAPTER 11

My summer runs of 2015 were some of the most youthful-feeling moments I'd had in a long time. I met Kaylee and the Desert Dash group every Wednesday. The group had a lot of regulars, and I got to know them. As the weeks went on, I ran with them instead of drifting away and running on my own. I learned about husbands and wives working together to take care of kids but still run. I learned about how some of them used running to lose weight and keep it off. I learned about hot yoga and how CrossFit was helping people get stronger. The conversations came easy and comfortable, and when my pace changed and I either pulled ahead or fell behind, no one cared. The group was easygoing and friendly.

I was feeling confident about group running now. My fears were all erased, so I decided to try another group I'd seen: Run Grrrls Run. They were meeting at a Starbucks for a morning run, so I headed to the location early that day. There was a sign for Starbucks inside a grocery store, so I sat outside in the parking lot and waited. And waited. And waited. There were no cars coming here, there were no runners hanging around. What gives? The meet time clearly had past, so I drove around trying to find some random runners. Nothing. Then I got around the corner and saw another Starbucks! Like, a big one in its own building. Of course, this was the right one. Who would have even found the other one? I messaged the group contact, Lisa, and told her my error. She must have thought I was an idiot; I certainly did. It was dark out, so I waited for dawn and chose another place to run.

Joining a second group had failed, but I was still enjoying the Desert Dash group. The trail had climbs that made me stronger, and I felt amazing—free and fast. Near the end of the summer, I had one run on that trail that reminded me of running when I was a kid. I was about three miles in, on the 601, which is an offshoot of the McCullough Hills Trail. I made a turn that sent me down the decent to the trailhead. The sun was just rising, and I fell into a rhythm that took me flying down. My steps glided from rock to trail to rock. They seemed to just float to where I needed them with just enough touch on the ground to propel me to the next step. It was the kind of running that made me feel like a gazelle prancing across the open plains, effortless and fast. It all just clicked, and I tried to memorize my gait so I could repeat it. When I got back to the trailhead, I looked at my time. I had run a mile in 8:05! That was incredible! I went to work that day feeling proud and excited to be a runner.

These runs continued late into the summer, but the mornings were getting dark. I started wearing a headlamp for the start of the run, and the sun was barely rising by the time we finished. I hadn't been able to repeat that amazing run, and since it was dark, I didn't want to push it and chance spraining my ankle or falling off the trail to a painful broken bone. I had to face the fact that these morning runs weren't going to happen all year; I had to find a new way to keep running. The warm summer mornings and the pleasant group of people made it easy to keep on schedule. If I wanted to be a runner through the winter, I needed something to motivate me: a goal, something so big that I had to stay on track. Then it came to me in a burst of resolution: I was going to run a marathon. I was closer than I'd ever been in my life to truly take on that goal. My knee pain hadn't been a problem lately, but my miles were low. If the pain did start up again, I could tough it out. Nothing was going to stop me—I was going to be a marathoner.

Now I had to figure out how to run a marathon. First, I needed a training program. Hal Higdon had worked for my half, so I printed out his marathon plan. I could pick a marathon anywhere in December or January; I could be ready by then. There was one in Portland, Oregon, where one of my brothers lives, and one in Spokane, Washington, where my sister lives. These would be perfect, but they were both in October, which was not perfect. There wasn't nearly enough time to be ready for them. Las Vegas had a marathon in November. Running the Las Vegas strip at night would be a cool experience, but a bulk of the run would be in neighborhoods just pounding out the miles in the dark. That was not the perfect experience I was looking for either. When I was a kid, I ran 10K races all the time, early in the morning, surrounded by spectators cheering us on. I wanted to relive that experience. How about the Chicago marathon? That's where I grew up. Then my mom, who got me started in running, could be there. But that was in October, too. I kept looking and found one in January, along the Pacific Coast, in Carlsbad, California. It wasn't too far; I could drive there. My mind was made up, I was going to run the Carlsbad Marathon.

The training schedule had me doing four days a week, but I was only doing three. My current schedule included runs of about five miles twice a week and one long run. At that point my long run was about ten miles. Now, I had to incorporate another day per week.

I decided to give the Run Grrrls Run group another chance. I looked up their Facebook page and saw a Thursday run scheduled at 5 a.m. at that same Starbucks. I chuckled as I pictured myself waiting in the empty parking lot. This time I would go to the right Starbucks. I had some of the same anxiety of group running that I did before I joined the Desert Dash group. What would these girls talk about? Would I have anything in common? However, the Desert Dash group was such a positive experience that I was fairly confident Run Grrrls Run would also exceed my expectations.

I got up early and arrived on time. I recognized Lisa, the

organizer, who made quick introductions. When 5 a.m. came, we promptly left. I was happy about that; another group that was respectful of everyone's time.

We headed out for our run with a pretty big group—about eight of us. Between the Desert Dash group, and now this group, I couldn't believe this many people were willing to get up at 5 a.m. to run. This was amazing! The pace and the route were both good, challenging but not too difficult. The girls were really friendly and I enjoyed chatting and running. When we were finished, we stopped at Starbucks and got coffees and chatted some more until it was time to go to work. If this group lasted, I had found my fourth running day. The Desert Dash runs were going to end at some point because of the dark early mornings. I would have to replace that run, but I wasn't going to worry about that just yet.

My weekday runs were going well, and I started watching the Facebook pages of these groups for weekend events. On Labor Day weekend, Desert Dash was hosting a group run at Bootleg Canyon, one of the trail systems in the valley. Kaylee and a few of the other runners I'd met over the summer were going. They were meeting early, which I liked, so I clicked the "Going" button.

I arrived at the meeting location and found a ton of runners. We headed out on the trails for the eight-mile run. I'd been consistently running five miles on the trails during the Wednesday morning runs, so eight was a stretch, but I felt confident at the start and was excited to see parts of this trail I hadn't ventured out on alone. We ran up a steep incline and at the top, the group waited for everyone. Then we headed out on a large loop on the backside of the mountain. It was wide open and just waking up to the morning sun. The Las Vegas strip in the distance looked small and contained. I thought about the first waggoneers who had traversed this land, back when it was the Wild West. I wondered how they could get this far without breaking down on the rough terrain.

My foot caught a rock in the path and I went nose diving

for the ground. I pulled my legs forward and regained my stride without falling. What a rough trail! I had recently noticed that I don't pick up my legs high enough. My gazelle-like trail legs had settled into more of a shuffle. This isn't a problem on road, but on the trails, it made it too easy to trip. I had to work on this. I continued down the trail, following the other runners. About a mile farther, my foot caught another rock. This time I couldn't get my legs under me in time.

"Oh, shit!" I yelled out. My chin smacked hard on a rock imbedded in the ground.

Jamie, a runner I'd met during my summer runs was by my side in an instant.

"Are you OK?" She asked.

"I think so, " I replied and smiled at the support.

Miraculously, my chin didn't hurt too bad, but my knee was cut open and bleeding. I thought about potential injuries and how this would affect my marathon training. Jamie offered water from her hydration pack to rinse it off. This sucked and I was in pain, but I couldn't help but think how lucky I was to be on a desert trail with someone I barely knew willing to help me. I got back up. I wasn't too far from the end of the route, so I was able to hobble back to the parking lot.

CHAPTER 12

The injuries from my fall at Bootleg Canyon weren't severe. I was healing up nicely and feeling badass that I'd have trail running scars. Things were in a good place for me. I had a goal—to run a marathon—and I was following a plan to make that happen come January. I also had groups to run with and was enjoying that. The Desert Dash group ended about a month into my marathon training as I expected it would. It had gotten so dark that the sun wasn't even up when the run was over. I didn't have any desire to run in the desert in the dark, but that left a gap in my running schedule. I had to pick up a fourth day again. I found another running group that met on Tuesdays at a local running shop. My fears of running groups were all but gone at this point, having been proven wrong twice now, so I wasn't concerned about meeting the new group. When I attended my first event I was again greeted with friendly running faces. Natalia organized the group and made me feel welcome. All paces were represented, and we waited at a few of the major turns on the route for everyone to catch up. It was an enjoyable and supportive experience.

I felt accomplished and goal oriented. Plus, my reasons for committing to running in the first place were accomplished. After that frightening day at work, I set my path on improving my health and I'd succeeded. It was a self-regulating thing: the more I ran, the easier it was to make better eating choices. My sugar shakes had completely stopped, and my ability to pass up the candy bowl was astounding. Not perfect but much better, and if I was running, I could take on a few sugar treats without much consequence.

So why was I on the Internet looking for a new challenge? Wasn't the marathon enough? Maybe it was because I always knew I would run a marathon, so having that as a goal was nothing new. I realized my searching wasn't about the running; something else was nagging me. I wanted to be part of something really interesting and challenging. I didn't want my life to pass by without me doing something really cool. By the time I was in my forties, I'd worked hard to get to a place where life was comfortable and easy. I had a good job and didn't have to worry about money too much, but it was easy to feel like I was in a rut. I felt a lot of pressure from books, news, and social media that I should pursue my passions and have a career doing what I loved. That my nine-to-five job was sucking the life out of me, and if I didn't quit and go down a path in life following my dreams, I would never be happy. When did nine-to-five jobs become something to resent? I just didn't think quitting my job to hustle for money was necessary nor that I would enjoy that path. I liked that my thoughts didn't swirl around money, that I could just enjoy this passion that I had to run and not have to make money from it. That would be too stressful. Nevertheless, I wanted to shake up my routine and feel like I was getting the most out of my life. The marathon was a great running goal, but I wanted something more adventurous, something that seemed impossible, something I could accomplish and then look back and say I did it.

What I really wanted was to be on *Survivor*—you know, the show where people wear the same clothes for a month without showers and vote each other off until one of them wins a million dollars. I'd only submitted applications repeatedly over the past decade. Once I even got a call from a recruiter for the show, Ken. He called while I was camping. It was meant to be! I was out of cell phone service and didn't get his voicemail until I was on the ride home. I started planning everything I needed to tell him. Once I got Ken on the line, I blurted out everything I could think of that might prove to him that I was worthy. Then he asked me where I lived and I said Florida.

"Oh," I heard on the other end of the line. *Crap, I'm losing him. No, no, NO! This is my chance. Quick,* I told myself. *Think of something!* But how could I talk my way out of where I lived?

"I love your energy; we always look for that in applicants. It's just that Florida is not my area. I'll pass your info off to the guy who covers that territory," and that's the last I ever heard from the show.

I had come to grips with the fact that *Survivor* might never happen for me and started scouring the Internet for other challenges. I liked the concept of *Naked and Afraid,* surviving in the wild and filming the experience. That seemed like a challenge most people wouldn't take on. After watching the show a few times, I decided I did not want to be naked with a stranger in the jungle, afraid of catching a waterborne disease from being too thirsty and tired to properly treat my water.

I'd always wanted to backpack across Europe or maybe South America, maybe I should plan a trip. How do you do that? How long would a trek take? Would there be a guide? How do you find a guide? Would I have to climb a mountain? I've always wanted to get to a mountain peak. How difficult is that? Can you breathe at the top of a mountain? Would I need one of those pickaxe-like tools and would I have to pull myself up the sheer face of a cliff using solely my arm strength? I flexed my bicep and squeezed it with my other hand, but there wasn't much muscle there. It all sounded so complicated, I didn't know where to begin to plan a trip like that.

Who was I kidding, how could I find the time for any of this? I had to work. I couldn't spend a month to be on *Survivor, Naked and Afraid,* or to backpack up a mountain. I couldn't fit any of this into my life until I retired. Then a simple question popped into my mind with such clarity that I couldn't believe I'd never thought of it before. Why would my life suddenly become adventurous when I retired if I wasn't adventurous now? I had to be the person I wanted to be now, and not burden my future with regret of all the things I didn't do. I couldn't wait until I retired and had time to get to all of the things I wanted to accomplish. I had to find the time and figure out how to start doing some of these things now.

I got back to my Internet search. I had to find a project that could give me an unbelievable adventure. I was on Facebook thumbing down my feed when a beautiful black-and-white picture of a snow-covered mountain caught my eye. The post read, "Becoming Ultra Season 2. Now accepting applications." It was listed in one of my running groups. I clicked on the post and read about an online podcast show that selected two average runners and documented their journey as they became ultra runners. *Ultra runner? What the heck is that?* I wondered. I read further to find out that anything over a marathon is an ultra, including trail races that spanned fifty to one hundred miles and more. I loved trails! This jogged my memory and I recalled a documentary I'd seen recently called *Desert Runners*. At the time, that kind of running seemed like something only elite athletes do, people with a ton of time and resources. It never dawned on me that I could do an ultra. In fact, as I watched the documentary, I wondered why anyone would bother to do it. When they faced hardships, I just thought, *Stop! You don't have to do this.* However, the scenery they ran the race in was awe inspiring. If ultra marathons were run in places like that, I should give it a shot.

The Becoming Ultra listing intrigued me. This sounded like the perfect challenge for me. Running was a thing I was doing already so I already knew the basics of racing and training, so it felt familiar and took away some of the fear of a new challenge. And although I was looking for a non-running goal, this offered so much more. The race promised a day full of adventure on the trails, a physical challenge that would push me harder than anything I had ever done, and with the podcasts, I'd have a unique form of documentation of the whole project. I read the criteria to apply. They wanted someone who represented an average runner, someone who had never run an ultra, someone who would keep in touch and record regular podcasts and post to social media, and someone who could be in Sacramento, California, in April 2016. I met all of these things. I wasn't sure how it would fit around my work schedule, hopefully I would get guidance from them. I could do this. They wanted the applicant to run a fifty-mile race. That had to be a typo. They couldn't get someone from thirteen miles to fifty in six months, could they? I blocked the reality of the distance from my mind. I was hooked, but I had to be selected. How could I show that I was everything they were looking for? I thought of my resume. I had never run more than thirteen miles in my life, but my recent half marathon time of three hours might scare them—granted it was a trail half and tough trail at that. I was a better runner now; I needed a better time. I searched for a half marathon and found the Saints and Sinners in Las Vegas. It was only a few weekends away, just before the application deadline, and it was all downhill. Perfect. I entered it immediately and started to write down all the reasons why Becoming Ultra needed to pick me.

The Becoming Ultra application consumed my every thought. I wrote pages of reasons why I should be selected and accomplishments I thought would convince them. Occasionally I thought about the fifty-mile distance, but I quickly tossed it into the back of my mind. I needed to focus on getting selected first.

I thought of what they would want in a candidate. I started to sort out my writings into my argument. One of the runners from the first season hadn't finished the training and didn't show up for the race. I emphasized how I wouldn't quit. And I wouldn't. When I put my mind to something, especially when I've made a commitment and someone is depending on me, I don't quit. I thought about the story they would want to tell. I was a runner from way back; when I was a kid I was a record breaker. I had won a few 10Ks and even a ten-miler. (Ask my mom; the way she talks about it, you'd think I was a superstar.) I even had my name in *Runner's World* magazine in 1984. It was just a blurb in the front, but I was twelve and had run a 10K in forty-two minutes. I wrote about my continued running as an adult, selecting a race every so often to give myself something to work for. Mostly just to stay fit. I also mentioned my knee pain, because they needed to know that it was there but I was willing to push through that and do what needed to be done. I wrote about finding a love for running again over this past summer. That it was beyond just exercise at this point and had become an activity I really enjoyed. I also mentioned my marathon goal; there was no way I was going to fail in that. From all of these things, they would see I wasn't a quitter, that I was the perfect candidate. I looked into the training for an ultra and found the maximum long run was thirty miles; I'd practically be there with a marathon. And the one I'd chosen was perfectly placed just a few months before the ultra.

The last thing I needed to do was get that better half marathon time. Talk is talk after all, and actions speak louder than words. The weekend of the Saints and Sinners Half Marathon arrived, and I showed up to the race and took a few selfies. I had to get used to that for the social media needs of Becoming Ultra. I got to the start line and pulled a wrap up over my knee. After the pain in my last half, I hoped this would help. The race started and I tried to go out slow, but the first part of this race was all downhill. My splits were fast, sub nine minutes for each of the first three miles. It was hot out and runners were complaining about that; many were from out of town and not used to the heat. I had been running in this weather, and I had a hydration pack, so I felt fine. We made a small loop out into the desert, and I noticed a few bighorn sheep whose path back up to the mountains was cut off by us runners so they were waiting patiently while corralled in a small valley. They were beautiful, and I pointed them out to a young man running next to me who was consumed in his own world with headphones and hadn't noticed them. I ran toward Lake Mead and then through the old railroad tunnels that serviced the Hoover Dam when it was being built. The course was beautiful, and I was feeling good. At mile ten, I did the math and if I pushed a consistent nine-minute pace, I could get a sub two-hour time. That would look great on the Becoming Ultra application. I picked up the pace. My last mile was a sub eight-minute mile! Unbelievable. I crossed the finish line just under two hours. I bent over and pressed my palms on my thighs. I pulled the wrap off my knee; it hurt pretty bad, but I finished and in good time. I was proud of myself and I fought back tears that overwhelmed me.

When I got home, I opened my application and found a place to brag about my race time. They also wanted a recorded voice message. I used the argument I'd written earlier to come up with a script to read. I recalled my *Survivor* application attempts and Ken, the *Survivor* recruiter, who said that they look for energetic applicants. I turned up my excitement, remembered to emphasize that I would never quit, and recorded a heartfelt message. I hit send. That was done. Adrenaline ran through my body. What if they picked me? In a way, of course, I wanted to be picked; this was that impossible thing I was looking for. The lazy part of my brain also wanted to know I tried my hardest and then not get picked, to not have to run fifty miles and go through the work to get there. I was sure there were other, more capable runners out there. I would go back to regular marathon training knowing I could have been a part of the Becoming Ultra project, but they just didn't pick me.

CHAPTER 13

The following week, Dan and I went to Zion National Park. We rented an RV and spent a few nights camping. We hiked up the river a few miles deep into the canyon. Most of the hike was in the river, so we used tall walking sticks for balance. I was glad for all the running I'd been doing; it made a hike like this easy. The canyon was beautiful, with steep walls creating shade on a hot day. That's what I wanted: to be fit and mobile enough to do things like this.

Later, we spent the night around the fire, cooking hot dogs and baked beans. I could eat like that once and a while because I was eating well most of the time—this was where I wanted to be. We set up a DVD player and watched a movie under the stars. Once we got tired, we retreated into the RV and snuggled with our dog. I slept hard after the day's hiking effort.

The next morning I ran from the campsite up a steep trail to a bluff that gave a nice view of the canyon. I stopped at the top feeling accomplished for making it up here. I didn't need a fifty-mile run for anything; doing things like this was what I wanted. I thought about just how far that would be to run, and then I laughed; that was just insane. I would spend the next few months preparing for the marathon, glad not to be facing that ridiculous distance. I felt strong and capable just the way I was. I was at peace.

When we returned home, I opened my email and there it

was: an email from Scott Jones of the Becoming Ultra project saying that they had chosen me as one of their runners to follow. My mouth dropped open as I stared at my computer. I was gonna run fifty miles? I was committing to unknown amounts of pain? Dan strolled in, taking a bite from an apple, and asked what was wrong. I looked at him, blank face, like a deer in headlights, and quickly lied.

"Hehe, you know, just another post about what someone had for dinner." I couldn't possibly tell him the truth. Could I? I needed some time to figure out what the hell I was gonna do about this.

I woke up the next day and opened my email again. It wasn't a dream: I had been selected for the Becoming Ultra project. A mix of anticipation, excitement, and fear brewed within me. Could I really do this? I was selected to be a part of this project, and I was excited about that. I didn't know a thing about running such a long race, but I hoped to get that kind of information from them. First up, I needed to bounce the idea off Dan.

I got up and went to the kitchen. Dan had made a pot of coffee so I poured myself a cup. When he came into the room, my heart skipped a beat. I've had crazy ideas before—like the time I told Dan we were going to be in a zombie movie. I had no problem telling him that. We were both excited and even got to go to a few read throughs before the project fell apart. At the time that project seemed pretty out there, so why was I having such a hard time telling him about the ultra? Because saying the words *fifty miles* and *I am going to run that far* was ridiculous. Best just to rip the Band-Aid off.

"So, I got selected for this project," I said.

"What have you gotten into now?" He smirked at me. He knew me so well.

"Well, it's this thing called Becoming Ultra," I said. I explained how I'd applied online and didn't think I'd get picked so I never mentioned it. I explained all the details. Well, all of them except the big one.

"OK, well, I'm sure you'll do great. How far is the race?" He took a sip of coffee.

"Um, like fifty miles, I think." I waited for his jaw to drop.

"That shouldn't be too bad. You just did thirteen. Fifteen should be no problem," he said.

"No, not fifteen. Fifty," I clarified.

"Fifty? That's like two marathons. You're crazy," he said.

"Well, I know," and then I tried to rationalize it as I'd been doing in my head. "I was going to run a marathon, anyway."

"Uh-huh," he said.

"The longest training run is only thirty miles," did I just say *only thirty miles*? "That's only slightly longer than a marathon."

Dan chuckled and smiled at me as he always does when I bring up a crazy idea. "Do your thing."

I was so lucky to have such a supportive husband. I feared this project would be a time consumer and I didn't want him thinking it was going to take over our lives, but he has always wanted me to pursue my whims. At least this one was keeping me in shape.

So now what? Dan accepted the idea of this project pretty easily. I was glad he had so much faith in me. I sent off an email to Scott to say that I was interested. He got back to me quickly to set up the taping session for the first podcast. He said that I would be running in the American River 50, as in fifty miles, and that he would cover the entry fee. I had to make my own arrangements to get to the race. He told me my assigned coach was Ian Sharman, and that I needed to contact him and work out payment for his services. He made it seem like I was commited already, but it all seemed to be happening too fast. I needed some time to think about all this. Fifty miles? Was that even reasonable? I thought about how I felt at the end of the half marathon I'd just finished. How was I going to do three more in a row? The idea was absurd. I had to make a pretty quick decision on this, once the podcast was taped, he would expect that I was planning to do this.

On my drive to work I looked across the valley and saw

Mount Charleston, the highest mountain in the valley, way out there in the distance. It took an hour to drive up there and that was fifty miles. *It isn't possible for me to run there, is it?* I looked back to the road and found myself a tire over the white line. I swerved to regain my lane. The truth was, I wasn't even sure I could run a half marathon twice to get to the marathon distance. My knee hurt with every step by the end of the Saints and Sinners half. But lots of people have run a marathon. I had to be able to do it, I just had to. Maybe the Becoming Ultra project was just what I needed to stay on track for my marathon goal. That was it: if I just focused on the marathon, I wouldn't have anything outlandish to concentrate on right now. The marathon was three and half months away, so for the bulk of the ultra training, I could just concentrate on the marathon and not be freaked out by the ultra distance.

If I decided to do this, then I would get coaching and maybe that was just what I needed to stay on track and actually run a marathon. I would have a professional to make all the training decisions and to reassure me. The Becoming Ultra project would keep me accountable and engaged. I decided that yes, I would do this project.

CHAPTER 14

With my decision made, I prepared for my conversation with the coach and for my first podcast. I googled my coach, Ian Sharman, and found out that he was an accomplished ultra runner. Like, really impressive. He'd run tons of ultras, some of them one hundred miles, and he'd won many of them. I couldn't fathom running one hundred miles, much less winning such a race. It would be good to have someone of that caliber in my corner.

I mentally prepared some questions about concerns that were on my mind. When I got on the phone with him, I couldn't remember any of them.

"What's your expectation for this race?" Ian asked in an endearing British accent.

I felt my eyebrows squish together. My expectation? I hadn't thought too much about that.

"To not die?" I said. He chuckled. Primarily, that was my concern, but I put a few more thoughts together. "I mean, to not get injured. I don't want any lasting internal or external injuries from this."

"OK," he replied.

I clenched my jaw. I expected more discussion on the matter. He sounded like my doctor who swiped away at the iPad because I hadn't yet mentioned anything that applied to the matter at hand.

"How time consuming is this going to be?" I asked. I feared that I'd be running ten miles five times a week and some insane long run.

"There's a time commitment, but it can fit into a normal schedule," he replied. I couldn't see how any of this would fit in. It seemed like way too much to accomplish. I had to trust that Ian knew what he was talking about.

He then talked about the longest training run of thirty miles. I thought about the eleven-mile loop around town that I'd run in preparation for my first half marathon. I thought about how long that took and how much pain I was in at the end. I'd have to do that three times in a row? How long would that take? Five hours? Six hours? Seven? That sounded crazy. I blocked it out of my mind. He talked about injury being the most important thing to watch out for and that I should tell him if anything hurt, even if it didn't seem too bad.

"Did Scott mention my knee issues to you? I told him about it in my application." Here we go, this was going to exclude me from this project. I was almost hoping it would be an out for me.

"Yes, that's something we need to watch. As the training progresses, keep me up to date about how it feels," he said. "Anything else?"

"Do you seriously think that fifty miles is something I can do?" I replied.

He let out a laugh and then said, "Yes. Your body can do more than you think it can."

He sounded very confident, like he was talking to a child standing on a diving board who just needs to believe it's not a big deal; then jumping becomes easy. Well, I guess I was jumping in.

I got a good feeling from Ian. His accent didn't make the fifty miles sound any more possible, but he seemed to share my philosophy on running. I feared getting a coach who would be too pushy with workouts, telling me to run through pain. He seemed just the opposite, very respectful of the task at hand and willing to make sure I didn't get injured.

The other runner selected for this project, Krystal, lived in Buffalo. I was glad not to be in her shoes; the thought of running through a winter there sent shivers up my spine. I wondered if we'd run together in the ultra or whether one of us would be faster. I imagined waiting for her to catch up at the aid stations. I'd be holding a cup of soup and offering encouraging words. Then I checked out Krystal's latest run on Strava. (For you newbies and non-runners, Strava is why you don't see a hundred posts of everyone's runs on Facebook. It is the Facebook for runners, where we list our runs, splits, elevations, kudos to each other. So if you're tired of seeing run info from your friends on Facebook, don't unfriend them; just tell them about Strava. You're welcome.) I realized she would probably be waiting for me. Krystal was fast. I mean, really fast. Like, her pace was better than my recent best, and she had done sixteen miles in a row that fast. I sighed. *I guess I'll be the underdog in this.* Then we met, and by met, I mean in the twenty-first-century social media kind of way. She's in the military and a part of Team Red, White and Blue, an organization that helps veterans by engaging them in physical activities with their communities. Krystal seemed really nice and helpful. We were gonna do well in this together.

So the coaching part was good and I met Krystal; now to meet Scott and do the first podcast. Scott and Ian had already taped a few episodes for Season 2 covering the plan for the season and choosing the runners for this season. He introduced Krystal and her coach, Liza Howard, in Episode 3. I would be joining the project in Episode 4. He planned to publish them as audio only podcasts, but was also taping it as a video chat, so I had to try to look nice and plan a background in my room. I angled my computer in such a way that behind me would be a blank wall. The time came for taping, so I called the number Scott had emailed me and started on my Becoming Ultra journey.

✻ ✻ ✻

Excerpt from the Becoming Ultra Podcast
Season 2 Episode 4
Meet Janet, Ian's runner for Season 2!
October 21

Scott: Welcome to Becoming Ultra, this is Scott Jones, your host, I am joined with coach Ian Sharman and Janet Patkowa. If you don't know what Becoming Ultra is, it's all things ultra running, with a little twist. We take a couple of runners who have never run an ultra and we take a couple of coaches who have run ultras at a very high level, and we coach them up and we share that whole journey, through podcasting and social media. We're gonna be sharing as much as we can over the next six months. The two subjects this year are Krystalore Stegner out of Buffalo, New York, and Janet Patkowa out of Vegas. If you're wanting to push the registration button on one of these big ultras, hopefully following these subjects will give you a little bit more courage to just dive in and just do it. Ian, on the spot, first impression of your new running client/athlete.

Ian: I think that the main thing is that Janet clearly is very committed to it and I think, if anything, I'll need to sometimes make sure that she has the flexibility to do things she needs to and not just do what I put on the plan regardless. I think she's gonna do really well.

Scott: Awesome. Janet, first impression.

Janet: I think that he's down to Earth, and sensicle, he definitely listened to my concerns and is more on the cautious, let's take it easy and make sure that you don't get injured, side, which was very important to me. I want to do this, but I want to enjoy it, I don't want to be in pain.

Scott: Ah, relative pain.

Janet: Yeah (*laughing.*)

Scott: Why did you apply to this project?

Janet: I saw the Becoming Ultra project posted in one of the many running groups on Social Media here in Vegas. It looked intriguing, and I was planning on running a marathon in January anyway, so I looked at what the training plans were for doing an ultra, and you get up to thirty miles. I know there's probably much more to it, but this is how I'm rationalizing it in my head right now. If I can get to the marathon, nothing is really going to change between then and now, just getting up to those miles, then I could probably do the ultra. And I thought the idea of having it all documented just sounded really cool.

Scott: Looking back to the application process, what are some things that you thought were interesting, that you thought would help, and what are some things that might hinder.

Ian: Janet came across as genuine and excited about the whole thing. I thought that Janet sounded like she really thinks of this as an epic challenge, which it is, and I think that would come across to people who are listening in on the live shows as well and I think that they would really appreciate that. We want to be really careful, of course, Janet's had some problems with her knee particularly when she's done the long run, so that is an area that's gonna be one of the most difficult things to work around where we want to be able to do a combination of making sure she has the right physical therapy and that she's working with people in person to make sure that the injury goes away. Ultimately we will need to gradually move things up over time, but there's no rush to do that just yet.

Scott: I need a prediction for how well Janet's gonna do in the American River 50.

Ian: It's just guess work at this stage. I will say this, she is going to finish, we'll know much more from how the marathon goes.

Janet: 10 hours and 36 minutes!

Scott: There we go, that's what I want.

Ian: I'll throw in a prediction... after the marathon.

Scott: Awesome. Janet, Ian, thanks for hanging out. Everybody else, you are listening to Becoming Ultra.

CHAPTER 15

Sensicle? Did I say *sensicle* in the podcast? That's not a word! I shook my head. These are going to be so embarrassing.

Scott had an upbeat personality and a positive demeanor, the kind of guy who made it sound like anything was possible if you just committed to it. He ran his own business coaching and encouraging athletes and the rest of us to take on the challenges we dreamed about. When Scott asked how long I thought fifty miles would take me, I guessed about ten and a half hours. *Could I run for that long?* Ian didn't wager a guess. I could only imagine what he was thinking: *This girl is never gonna finish this race. What is she thinking? She's never even run a marathon!* Well, those were my fears anyway.

After we finished taping the first episode, Scott, Ian and I worked out a time for the next taping. Scott wanted to have an interview with Ian and me for updates on my progress every two weeks all the way to the fifty-miler. He would also be doing the same with Krystal and Liza on the alternating weeks. So I would be taped in all of the odd-numbered episodes, and Krystal in all of the even-numbered episodes. Scott told me that the podcast would be posted on the Becoming Ultra website. *Who would listen to these podcasts and how it would help them?* He told me to post often on the Becoming Ultra Facebook page to update his followers about my progress. I was excited about interacting with people who would be following along; I hoped to get encouragement to get me through this project.

The only thing left to do was start training. For my first week, my long run was a fourteen-miler, only a mile longer than my longest. I set out on a tough stretch of trail, Amargosa. There were lots of steep inclines and declines and I should have stayed away from it for this long run, increasing my miles was challenging enough and there were easier trails in the area. But I was feeling strong and confident and I wanted to start this training with an accomplishment that would make me feel like the ultra runner I had signed on this project to be. Afterward, my knee was killing me; I'd forgotten my knee wrap. I also had a new pain in the side of my foot. I looked at my Nike trail shoes and wondered if they were part of the problem. Pam, a runner from the Run Grrrls Run group, had the same shoes and had run lots of tough trails in them, so I thought they would be fine. Maybe they just weren't right for me. Or maybe that stretch of trail was just too challenging for me. It was way too steep to be doing my long run on it. *What was I thinking? I was in way over my head with this project. I am no ultra runner.* I was humbled and felt deflated. I decided to forget about this trail for the duration of my training. I logged my miles when I got home, then went on the Internet and ordered some new shoes. The next weekend was a fifteen-miler—again, the longest run of my life. I chose a route that was much less demanding. No need to stress my knee that bad.

The day of the fifteen-miler, I loaded up my hydration pack, grabbed my knee wrap, and put together some snacks before heading out. About two miles in I ran into two older fellas on short bikes—the kind where you lay back and extend your feet out in front. The whole device looked tailor made to kill your back.

"Well you're a serious runner, aren't you?" One of them shouted as they passed me.

I suppose if I didn't know me I'd say the same thing. I had a military-style backpack strapped on. By military, I mean there are pockets for everything and enough water to cross the

Sahara, or at least this side of town, hopefully. But I didn't feel serious; I just felt free. Free to know that I could do anything I wanted to, or at least try to, anyway.

So I answered the man down there on the back-killing machine by saying, "Just prepared."

The sun was coming up over the horizon and it was sure to be blazing in no time.

Most of the run went fine. My knee hurt but the wrap was helping; I wore it around my ankle and pulled it up when I felt like I needed it. *Tough it out,* I told myself. *This is what it's about, right? There's no time for an injury, so I must keep going.* By the time I got to fifteen miles, I dreaded each time my left leg banged the pavement and sent an increasingly sharp pain to the base of my knee cap. I finished and didn't think I could walk another step, much less run more. Fifty miles? That would be another thirty-five miles. I might as well have been thinking about building my own spaceship and visiting an alien planet. I had no way of connecting that many miles to my body's ability to run it.

I got home, logged my miles, and sent an email to Ian with an update. Ian would be proud. I was on schedule and doing the miles I was being asked to do. I sat back with an ice pack on my knee and a pint of ice cream in my hands, and waited for a response from Ian.

When it came, I opened the email and read, "Go see a physical therapist."

CHAPTER 16

No, no, no! I'm fine. I can take the pain. I don't have time to mess around with physical therapy. I wondered how many visits it would take to fix this and how much that would cost. I couldn't be worrying about this. I had to get my miles up. Scott and Ian were going to regret picking me; how could they not? I was already having problems and we'd just started.

However, I couldn't deny that Ian was right. I needed to get this knee issue straightened out once and for all. I probably should have already gone to see someone. It wasn't that I didn't want to; I would actually welcome someone watching me run and telling me what I was biomechanically doing wrong so I could fix it. But I was scared. A physical therapist would just want me to take time off, rest it, ice it, and for goodness sakes, never run again because it's so bad for the knees! I didn't want that diagnosis and I couldn't afford to take a bunch of time off.

I needed to find a physical therapist who knew about running. Someone who at least understood that running is good for a body. Did this type of physical therapist exist? I was glad I'd joined some running groups in town because now I had some people to ask. Surely, I wasn't the first to have this kind of issue. I posted on one group's Facebook page and got lots of responses. Runners in town were happy with two therapists in particular, and their praise of these two people was amazing—stories of pains that had been fixed. My spirits lifted. I did some recon on the therapists' websites. I got excited: both of them were runners and worked with runners to keep them running. One was on my insurance, and the other didn't seem too expensive.

I chose the one that was not on my insurance. A therapist tied to an insurance company would be required to follow protocols, and I needed someone who could work outside of those restrictions to solve my problem better and faster. It cost more than I wanted to pay, but not unreasonable. I was already paying for coaching and I didn't like spending more money for this project, but I had to make a decision: how important was running and moving around in general? This was my chance to finally see if my knee was fixable. It inhibited me and kept me from making goals that I wanted to achieve. I had wanted to run a marathon, but my knee pain was always in the back of my mind, so I'd put off the decision to do it for years. Now, I was committed to running a marathon and an ultramarathon and the whole Becoming Ultra project. I had to put the cost of therapy in the bigger picture. If it was all a waste of money and my knee was screwed, I'd at least know I did everything I could. However, what if I went through the therapy and my knee pain went away? What would I be capable of then? Would the money be worth having a fixed knee? I knew other runners had been helped by this therapist, so I decided to go for it. I certainly couldn't continue with Becoming Ultra if I didn't. Ian wasn't going to let me keep on a training schedule if I kept reporting back that my knee hurt and I wasn't doing anything about it.

So I called and made an appointment.

A few days later, I pulled into the parking lot of Maximum Velocity Physical Therapy. This was it: I was finally going to get a professional opinion on my knee. I was anxious about what this person would say. Would I be on a road to repairing it? Or would I finally have to accept that my knee was going to be something that would always impair my activities? I just wanted to get this over with.

I went inside and met Ron Gallagher. We discussed what

was going on and where I was having pain. He watched me run, and we went over what he saw. According to Ron, my problem was typical. Over the course of my life, my body had moved using the least amount of energy possible. This caused me to develop harmful habits like bending over for things instead of squatting and leaning into my hips when I stand. As a result, I'd changed the way I walked and ran, and the muscles in my body were all imbalanced. It was pretty obvious that my form was all over the place, but Ron gave me good news: it was fixable. He said that because my muscles weren't built up—namely, my quads, hips, and glutes—my body was compensating and my form was suffering as a result. So I was landing and placing unneeded stress on my knees. This all made sense. I'd already noticed how building up my muscles had helped with my lower back pain; it only made sense that my knee pain would have the same solution. I was aggravating the problem when I ran and when I went about my day-to-day activities. My muscles were just getting weaker and weaker since I never required them to chip in fully. First and foremost, he said there was a simple fix and I didn't have to stop running. In fact, stopping running would be the worst thing to do. As my body got stronger, it needed the motion and stress to get better and relearn how to work right. If this physical therapy worked, it would help on such a wider level, beyond just running.

He laid out a plan for the next three weeks, thinking that by then I would have built the muscles necessary to go forward without pain. We did some exercises and weight-loaded movements. The big one was squats. I needed to be doing them with weight to make my legs stronger; running alone wasn't doing enough. Ron had me squat with a barbell on my shoulders. Just the barbell, no weights. He said it weighed about thirty-five pounds. I could barely do it. He said eventually I would be able to do this with my body weight on it. Ha! Do this with another one hundred pounds? Yet another impossible thing. I knew this would require a lot of work and wouldn't come quickly, but I was encouraged.

I got back in my car and cried. A weight had been lifted from my shoulders—not just the barbell but also the imagined one. Because I'd already had surgery and still had pain, I'd been thinking this was just the way my knee was going to be. Learning that wasn't true was a huge relief. Plus, I always thought that physical therapy would mean I had to stop running altogether. Or that fixing my knee would be so expensive it wasn't even worth starting. Now I knew that wasn't the case. I should have done this years ago. Big lesson learned from this project: don't be afraid of what I don't know. Get all the information; it may not be nearly as awful as I think.

After I got home, I sent an email to Ian telling him I had an answer and that I was ready to get going on this training because everything was gonna be OK.

"Whoa, slow it down," he replied and reminded me that I hadn't actually fixed anything yet. Oh yeah, that. Training was like slowed time, and my brain was fifty steps ahead of what my body could do. And all I could do was wait.

* * *

Excerpt from the Becoming Ultra Podcast
Season 2 Episode 5
The best ways to deal with early potential injury
November 6

Scott: Hey, welcome to Becoming Ultra. You guys are following Janet and Ian as he coaches her up for a fifty-miler in April. When injuries are showing up early on, what do you do, what is the strategy when you know you're gonna go through with it?

Janet: Well, my knee hurts when I run too far. I don't want to go see a physical therapist, because they're gonna tell me to stop running. But I logged a couple of long runs, and Ian said to go see somebody. So I went to see someone, he said my problem is pretty common when your muscles aren't built up. He gave me a couple of tips of things to change, and the physical therapy sessions are focusing on strengthening the muscles that aren't built up enough. It's not an instant fix, I can see some improvement, I can see some promise, but there are definitely some muscles that need to get built up before my legs can take the shock that they are supposed to.

Ian: And it's setting you up for the long term. Not just this fifty-miler, but to be able to keep enjoying running for decades because this is an area where if you hadn't of gotten it fixed, it would probably just keep being an issue. It wasn't a surprise that we needed to deal with this but it's good that you went to someone who knows what they are talking about and he's been able to look at you run and not just see the symptoms, but to get to the root of the problem. It's the kind of thing that lots of people deal with and without correcting and making sure that the body and the biomechanics are working efficiently, every time you try to increase the mileage, it's likely to lead to problems. The fact that we've identified this at pretty much six months from the race gives us loads of time to be able to build up gradually and injury free.

Scott: Three things, if you do these things you're less likely to start out with injury. First thing, train like an athlete. Don't just run, increase range of motion and strength. Second, change only one variable at a time when you're increasing load or volume. Third thing, don't fear information from a professional.

Scott: Thank you guys for listening to Becoming Ultra, until next time, I'm Scott Jones, with Ian Sharman and Janet Patkowa.

CHAPTER 17

I saw Ron twice a week and we worked at strengthening my muscles. I saw great improvements. I had runs where my knee didn't hurt, and then runs where it did. Ron kept telling me that it would happen soon and I wouldn't think about my knee anymore. I hoped he was right; I wanted him to be right, but the pain persisted albeit inconsistently. I was ready to be done with this, but my body wasn't there yet.

I was doing box jumps at his facility one day when I was tired from work and didn't care to try very hard. I was landing hard on the box, and Ron stopped me.

"Wait," he said. "I want you to think about the race. How do you think you'll fix this at thirty miles in if you can't do it right now?"

That hit hard. I knew I was slacking off mentally, but I didn't think it showed physically. The work wouldn't get done because I showed up; it would get done when I put in the effort. I needed to focus on every move, every time, or not bother at all.

I had some great runs after that, moments when I really thought I had beat my knee pain. Then one day, I was doing a long run, out and back on a mountainous desert trail. To get to the halfway point, I climbed to a saddle, down a small valley, up switchbacks to the highest point, and then down toward a park on the other side of town. I then turned around and went back up to the highest point and headed down the switchbacks.

That's when I couldn't deny it anymore: my knee hurt like it did in the half marathon trail race in May and like it did in my sub-two-hour Saints and Sinners half in September. *How can this be?* I had to stop because it hurt so bad. *What am I going to do?* I looked around and found myself at the bottom of a valley. I was four miles from my car and could hardly walk. I checked for snakes under a large lava rock at the side of the trail and then plopped down on it. I put my head in my hands and stared at my knee. I sat there for a while, wondering how I would get back, and all I saw around me were mountains and desert.

I pulled the wrap from my ankle over my knee. Getting some pressure on it made it feel better. What about all the work I'd done? When was that going to work? Why wasn't this better yet? I was so far into training and hadn't even run my marathon yet. What would Scott and Ian say when I told them I still had knee pain? They kept saying there's plenty of time, but it seemed like time was slipping by and I was never going to get rid of this pain.

I started to walk my way out of the valley. Within a short distance, I started to run and felt good enough to continue. Maybe Ian was on to something when he said, "Your body can do more than you think it can."

The next week I went running with my friend Jamie, who had helped me at Bootleg Canyon when I'd fallen. We went to Blue Diamond, a small town on the west end of the valley. As soon as we started our ten-miler, I heard a pack of coyotes howling. I smiled and looked around but saw nothing. There was no way to know how close they were; the sound was no doubt bouncing off the nearby mountains. As I listened to them yip and howl to each other, I felt a warmth brew inside of me, a feeling of connection to the world I live in. I had seen many unusual things while I was out running, like the previous summer when the presidential motorcade passed me at Lake Las Vegas. I had peered into black windows to see which car the president was in, but I couldn't tell. Another time I watched a jack rabbit race for its life to get away from a coyote. I wouldn't have seen any of this if I was safely sitting at home, protecting my knee.

It made me mad that I had been missing out on accomplishing things because of my knee pain. It was always on my mind and limited how much I thought I could run. Before the Becoming Ultra project, I kept my mileage per week low so that my knee wouldn't hurt, but that only stopped the symptom of the problem. It never solved the problem of what was causing it. But now that I was trying to get my body to do so much more, I couldn't hide from the pain. I was forced to figure out how to fix it. If I learned to move by using my muscles properly, I would be so much better able to run and move in general. Maybe my pain wasn't some mysterious, unknown thing about getting older that I just had to accept, but instead a sign to get off my ass and do something about it.

I finally knew what people meant when they said, "If you want to do a big project, you need to ask for help." With the Becoming Ultra project, help was put in my lap. It wouldn't have occurred to me to hire a coach, and I wouldn't have gone to a physical therapist either. I knew my running gait was poor, but I didn't know how to begin to do anything about it. Nothing beats professional help from people who actually know what they are talking about.

Things changed for me by getting help. I had feared running long distances was going to have catastrophic consequences and that I would injure myself beyond repair, but that fear subsided. Following a plan that's being managed by someone else was great for two reasons. First, the plan would get me prepared without me having to figure everything out. That was the purpose of having a coach. A coach has seen others through this process and knows what's possible. Second, I didn't have to picture the whole project from start to finish. If I had to look at the immensity of the entire project, it'd be too overwhelming. It was much easier to just look at the next few weeks—that was the extent of the training plan Ian gave me at one time.

* * *

Excerpt from the Becoming Ultra Podcast
Season 2 Episode 7
New tools for the runner training for her first Ultra
November 20

Scott: Hey, welcome to Becoming Ultra. I'm your host Scott Jones and I'm here with Ian Sharman and his awesome runner, Janet Patkowa out of Vegas. Today we're going to talk about some of the new tools Janet's been using with her running. So let's do a quick catch up for Janet. Ian gave her the advice to go to a PT. Ian's not in the same town as her, he can't go and do a gait analysis. The basics, she was weak, she needs to increase the strength.

Ian: Most importantly, it's where the weaknesses were, and what exercises would fit and that's where a specialist can really help. What are the specifics about the way Janet was running that were causing problems and which muscles needed to be strengthened. I think Janet's really noticing it day by day; you're starting to see it feeling more normal, feeling stronger.

Janet: The last couple of weeks have been really encouraging, and at the same time incredibly frustrating. I feel like I'm doing everything my PT is asking and at the same time, some runs are really great, and some are like I haven't been doing anything. It's good that I'm dealing with someone who's a professional in that area, because you get so many doubts. I can ask him specific, it's still hurting, and where do we go from here. He can then tweak those exercises to make it better. We're getting there, not completely there yet, but there's definite promise.

Ian: Do most of the runs feel better at this stage?

Janet: Yes, for sure.

Scott: Other athletes are going through this right now. Try to look at the big picture, over the long haul, am I getting better? If the answer is yes, then keep moving forward.

Ian: We have a six month period to build up to American River 50. We have to go back to basics; we still have plenty of time.

Scott: Coach to student runner, Janet, you have a half marathon tomorrow, Ian, what's the advice?

Ian: We've had several weeks with fifteen-, sixteen-milers, so this is a little shorter. It's a chance to practice that race environment. It's very much about doing your own race, and that's one of the key skills that we'll need for the ultra. You have to be able to judge early on what's sustainable.

Scott: What are some new tools that Janet is using?

Janet: I have a metronome that beeps at me as I run and I try to hit a foot every time I hear it.

Ian: Various studies have shown that a cadence of 180 is the most efficient. If you're forcing yourself to quicker steps, you don't have as much time to over stride and put your leg too far in front because there's no time to do that.

Scott: What other tools are you using?

Janet: One is more of a mental tool. I need to have the form down. I need to be working on all these things at mile one or two, when everything is easy, if I think it's all going to come together when I'm exhausted and I'm trying to keep going step by step, it isn't going to happen. If you go to the gym to do push-ups, do five right instead of pushing to do ten wrong.

Ian: You want to reinforce the good form, if you do it with bad form, all you're doing is reinforcing bad habits. An ultra runner's tool kit isn't just the gear they use, it's really a whole set of skills that you develop overtime that is internal.

Scott: Guys, thanks for joining me today, it was fun. Good luck tomorrow on your half.

CHAPTER 18

In late November, I had two races scheduled. I planned both before joining the Becoming Ultra project, and Ian said it was fine to run them. My knee was on my mind, but I was doing the work my physical therapist prescribed and I wasn't going to let the fear of pain stop me. First up was a Desert Dash trail race, Trails of Glory. I signed up for the half marathon as a way of revisiting my challenge from earlier in the year. I wanted to see how much I'd improved. Later in the week was the Turkey Trot, a 12K at the old railroad tunnels that lead out to Hoover Dam. I tried to run a Turkey Trot on every Thanksgiving Day. Maybe half my adult years I actually did it, and sometimes I was prepared for it, sometimes not. I remember doing Turkey Trots as a kid on freezing cold Illinois mornings, and doing them as an adult made me think of those days with my family. I was looking forward to it this year. With all my training, I didn't think I would have problems with a 12K. If my knee pain flared, I would just have to deal with it.

For the Trails of Glory race, I decided to volunteer at packet pickup. Since the Desert Dash runs over the summer had helped me so much, I wanted to give back to this group. Volunteering also came with race credit for the future, so it was truly a win-win. I sat behind the table and handed out race bibs and swag bags. Runner after runner stepped up, and I got to meet those who would be out on the course with me. Managing a line of people quickly took more multitasking than I was expecting, and I channeled my dormant inner bartender. I was a natural at this. I smiled, gave short instructions, and sent runners on their way. Afterward, I went home to make final preparations for my race.

The next morning, I showed up early. A chill greeted me when I opened the car door. I shivered and wanted to put on a sweatshirt. I knew it would warm up soon so I let my brain manage my clothing choices. I headed to the start line. It was still twilight; the sky was clear and it looked like once the sun came up, it was going to be a nice day.

When the race started, I tried to hold back. Ian told me to take it easy in the beginning and try to keep a consistent pace throughout. I wanted to do that, but this first mile felt so easy. It was downhill and I flew. After a few miles, the course headed uphill and I still felt good, so I pushed hard on the uphills. About the halfway point, Cheyenne and Sanja, two friends from the Run Grrrls Run group, were manning the aid station in their PJs, so I stopped and chatted for a moment. Then I pressed on. The course continued uphill until about a mile from the end, and then there was a downhill that headed for the finish. I had energy left and flew the last mile. I finished around two and a half hours. That was a half hour quicker than the race at the beginning of the summer, and even though this was a different course, I still blew away my time. My knee hurt, so I put on my wrap after the race was over. Regardless, I felt proud and accomplished.

Later that week, I headed to the Turkey Trot. I was halfway to the race when I noticed I'd forgotten my watch. That was a bummer; my watch gave me a real-time pace as I ran. Ian had told me that pacing should be done by effort, so this would be a chance to try that out.

I parked and hiked down to the crowded start line; I felt anxious. The race started and I sped through the first half. By the second half I was working hard to maintain a decent pace. My knee hurt with each step, and the crowded course never spread out. The finish line was confusing with people who'd already finished being allowed to use the race course as a path back to their cars. At one point I had to stop so as not to run into a group that crossed my path. When I finished, my time proved a good effort, but I felt unsettled about it.

Two race efforts in one week was too much. My knee hurt and I'd pushed too hard. I didn't get my normal nostalgia reaction to the Turkey Trot. I was irritated and just wanted to go home.

When I got there, Dan and I worked together to get a turkey feast prepared. Our place filled with the familiar aromas of many Thanksgivings. We got on the computer and did a video chat with my family. My mom and dad were at my brother's home in Chicago, my sister tuned in from Washington, and my other brother logged in from Oregon. We didn't do much catching up because my nieces and nephews goofed around and every time they made noise, the computer changed whose microphone was turned on. It was still comforting to see everyone and share a few moments since they were all so far away.

Later that day, Dan and I watched football and enjoyed our feast. I thought about all of the training I had done, and all that was left to do. Looking ahead on the schedule was daunting. Every time I looked to see how the miles were piling up, I panicked about running fifty miles. I took a deep breath and reminded myself that I wanted to run a marathon, so I would have been doing this anyway. I was running over thirty miles per week—not breaking any records, but this was more than I had ever run.

The Becoming Ultra project was testing me and seeing what I was really capable of doing. What could the future bring if I opened myself up to new challenges, maybe not all the scripted ones? Maybe that's why the Turkey Trot was disappointing. I was trying to hang on to a feeling of the past. I needed to move forward to the challenges of the future and not push to hold on to the way I used to do things. The fifty-miler was an opportunity to do that, but the whole project was just too big to think about in its entirety. I had to remember that this project wasn't going to get done in one day. It took time and I had to trust the process.

My future was now going to exist in short increments. I couldn't manage the whole training program in my head, I couldn't even think too much about the number *fifty*, so focusing on short increments was the best idea for me. November was over, and I looked ahead to December. In the first week, I had a seven-miler scheduled for Tuesday and a six-miler on Thursday, but the groups I ran with on Tuesday and Thursday only ran five miles. I would have to run the extra miles before the groups showed up, but that would mean running alone, in the dark. The hairs raised on the back of my neck.

I stopped at a Fry's Electronics to buy a camera card, and at the counter I saw pepper spray in a small pink canister. I bought it. Would this save my life? I doubted it. I opened the package, held the canister in my hand, and thought, *this is supposed to keep me safe?* I imagined a creeper jumping out from the bushes and me handily spraying him in the eyes and then running to safety. More likely, he'd scare the crap out of me and I'd drop the canister and stumble to the ground. At least it was something.

On Tuesday, I layered up for the cold temps and donned the canister, my weapon of spray. I showed up about twenty minutes early and ran loops around the parking lot, canister in hand. Whole Foods was receiving deliveries, and I watched the guys unloading the truck; no need to spray them. I ran to a more secluded area of the parking lot and carefully watched stray parked cars, giving them a wide berth. When I hit two miles, I returned to the running store where the morning group was assembling. I tossed the canister in my car and joined the group. We set out for five easy-paced miles, but I needed a progression speed run which is exactly what it sounds like: start easy and gradually increase throughout and finish feeling pretty fast. So I set out with the group, but pulled ahead of most of them within the first mile. It was comforting that so many runners were out that early, but I didn't get to run or converse with anyone so these were still lonely miles.

I got home and logged my miles. I looked ahead to the month of December and saw all of the long weekday runs. My heart sank. Even though I knew these weekday runs were necessary—that if I didn't do them, I'd never be ready for the upcoming twenty-milers—thinking about all of those runs and all of the parking lot miles was too much. It did nothing but fuel my overwhelmed feeling. I told myself to calm down. Running lots of miles through the cold winter was just part of it. I reminded myself to think in small increments so I only looked ahead to my next run: a seven-miler on Thursday. I would show up early, canister in hand, and run two miles before the morning group arrived.

On Thursday, I arrived at Starbucks' dark parking lot twenty minutes before I was to meet the Run Grrrls Run group, and I ran up the street alone toward a school about a mile away. When I got there, I saw numerous emergency phones throughout the parking lot. The ones you hit a button on if someone is chasing you. I remembered seeing phones like these all over campus when I was in college. They were supposed to make you feel comforted that help was only a push of a button away, but I still felt vulnerable being out here alone in the dark. I looked at my pink canister and did not get the reassurance I was hoping for. My watch signaled a mile, so I turned around.

When I got back to Starbucks, the girls were assembling. The group was usually the same, although some people came just for a run or two, and then I never saw them again. We set out for our run and chatted; my fears of getting chased subsided. When we were done, we sat and had coffee. This had become my favorite run of the week. These girls showed up week after week, and I became friends with all of them. They were an incredible group of runners who were also interesting and fun to talk to, like Connie, who was taking voice-over lessons, and Kelly, who was getting a master's in chemistry. I had a chemistry degree, too, so we geeked out on molecules. I told Ian that whatever he put on the schedule, it had to fit in with this group.

A few days later, I got a Facebook post about Lisa, the group organizer. She was moving and her going away run was a few weeks away. They were meeting on the Las Vegas strip and doing a road run from there. It sounded like fun, and I wanted to go, but I was on a schedule. I looked at my training plan. I had a trail run scheduled that day! My shoulders slouched and I frowned through tight-pressed lips. *You've got to be kidding me.* I clicked the "Can't attend" button and slammed the lid of my laptop shut.

* * *

Excerpt from the Becoming Ultra Podcast
Season 2 Episode 9
Adjusting to the miles (mentally), life/running balance, and mandatory runs for the world
December 4

Scott: Hey, welcome to the Becoming Ultra show. You guys are gonna hear Ian and Janet today. This is the most she's run in her life and she's still intimidated. I also want to talk about work/life balance, and how are we balancing that.

Why don't you talk about what's been on the regimen of your training since we talked last.

Janet: I had two races, the trail half marathon, and that same week, on Thanksgiving day I had the Turkey Trot which was a 12K. So it's been a lot of stress on my body and I'm trying to work that in with the physical therapy sessions and I'm like oh my gosh is my body going to be able to take this. The marathon is in about a month and a half. I'm really trying to trust in the schedule that Ian has set up for me. Keeping in communication with him about how I'm feeling.

Ian: I think the basic thing is that we're trying to gradually build up the mileage. The main thing is making sure that she gets the time on feet and that the knee isn't a problem. The pace of the marathon is pretty much irrelevant. We just want to have the marathon itself to be something she's able to get through, uninjured. She'll get confidence, it'll be a great training run, both physically and tactically for the ultra, another three months down the line.

Scott: I know when I was training for a first marathon, or even the first time I ever ran ten miles, to have the confidence to go from one to ten was huge.

Ian: A month down the line, your body's adapted, and suddenly these things become possible. I think at this point for Janet it's just realizing that each time she's doing each of these long runs, each time she's gradually building up the mileage, her body is reacting to that. It's being forced to adapt. What seems kind of almost impossible at this point, then becomes much more reasonable.

Scott: Sixteen miles is not like an hour and a half of Janet's morning, it's a big chunk of her weekend, so let's talk about some legitimate tactile advice for people on how to do these things and still maintain healthy relationships and healthy time with people you care about.

Ian: One of the main things is letting the person know what commitment you're putting into the running so they're not always thinking you're doing more than they expected. The other thing is trying to fit it in the most convenient time. So that you're thinking what fits in best for the family, and not just yourself.

Janet: It's time management, I look at the weeks as separate entities. Instead of looking at, always on Tuesday's I'm gonna do this at this time, I think this is this week, what do I have going on and what's going to fit in.

Scott: The last question, Janet, you've said that running makes you a happier person, and I 100 percent agree with that, and there's physiology that backs that concept. So here's a hypothetical question, if everyone in the world was forced to run three to ten miles every single morning before they left their house, what would the world look like?

Ian: I think that a lot of people would make that their commute. I think that the world would be a better place. Although I'm not sure you'd want to do that in a war zone.

Scott: Thank you guys for listening to the Becoming Ultra show.

CHAPTER 19

I can still hear the question asked by many non-running friends: "Why are you doing this?" This was usually followed by, "I could never do that." Some days, I wanted to be that person, the one who wouldn't do this. I had to remind myself of why I was doing this: I wanted something to focus my attention on, an impressive challenge that I could accomplish. But then I would start doubting again and wonder what my accomplishment would do for anybody. It was kind of selfish, really, in that it was time consuming and I wasn't helping anyone or my community. However, I had made a commitment to do this for myself and for Scott's Becoming Ultra project. I wanted to complete the fifty-miler and see how achieving that would change me.

Parts just weren't fun, but they were necessary. I was intimidated, even scared, by the twenty-miler I saw on the schedule. My knee was finally calming down, but twenty miles was going to be a huge stress on it—on my whole body. And yet, it still wasn't near the 26.2 miles of a marathon. After the twenty, how would I possibly be able run a whole 10K? I wondered how a few twenty-milers would be enough preparation.

On the morning of my first twenty-miler, I set up my hydration pack with two liters of water, and I packed dried cranberries and two homemade sweet potato mixes into one of the many pockets of my pack. The sweet potato mixes were a homemade mash I was trying as an alternative to the manufactured energy gels that were on the market. I made these with sweet potato, honey, and sea salt then packed the mash into a zip lock bag. When the clock ticked 5:45 a.m., I grabbed everything and drove to a small park near my house where I met Kaylee; she was going to run the first part with me.

I felt good at first, but I also knew the pace was probably too fast. During the summer trail runs, I had no problem keeping up with her. But this was early in a very long run. After six miles, Kaylee was done, so I said good bye and continued on.

With Kaylee I averaged mid- to low-nine-minute miles. Almost immediately after she left, I fell to a mid-ten- to eleven-minute pace. That was more maintainable. The time and the miles passed. I was on a route through town and was impressed with myself when I saw how far I was from the mountain I lived at the foot of.

At the top of every hour, I took out my sweet potato mix and ate it by squeezing it out of the zip lock bag. It took several minutes to eat the whole thing because I didn't stop running. On the half hours, I ate some cranberries. Those were easier to manage.

My knee started to hurt after about fourteen miles. I thought back to the early, fast miles and wondered if my knee would be hurting less if I had gone slower. *Too late now*, I mused. I also thought about the physical therapy and the Becoming Ultra project. Without Ian, I wouldn't have gone to PT. Sure, my knee hurt, but I knew it was getting fixed; I just wasn't all the way there yet. Without the project, I would have wanted to quit so as not to hurt myself. But now, it was like blind will. I was doing it no matter what. I promised them I would finish an ultramarathon, and I wasn't going to go back on my word.

The miles got progressively more difficult, and by the time I was done, I was done. My muscles burned and my knees throbbed. I still had a little more than a month until the marathon. I couldn't see walking much more, much less running more. I wasn't happy with the pain I felt, and seeds of doubt started springing up; a little voice asked, "Why are you doing this?" But I rejected it. I wasn't going to quit. I was going to stick to the training plan without question. In a month, the marathon would be behind me and I could start concentrating on the ultramarathon. I didn't see how I was going to get to the finish line of the marathon much less the ultra, but so far, I had done everything Ian said I could do. I put my trust in him and hobbled home to get some ice on my legs.

When I had run seventeen miles the week before, I had worried about the pain level during a marathon—if I was already in a fair amount of pain, what would it be then? What would happen to my knee? After that seventeen-miler, I was still nine miles away from marathon distance, and I still had a lot of uncertainty about the condition my body would be in after another nine miles. Now that I had run twenty, some of my anxiety dissipated. Now a marathon was only six more miles. I reasoned that the pain I felt at the end of twenty was about what I'd feel at the end of the marathon. I could see that, yes, my knee hurt, but I could finish this. I really could. Yes, it would hurt, but I would be OK. This was the pain I had worried about, and it was not that bad. I knew I was gonna survive.

A few days after the twenty-miler, I had a scheduled physical therapy appointment. When I arrived, I set about doing all the exercises that Ron had taught me. As I made the circuit, I thought about my knee pain and this therapy. It was helping and I believed it was the solution, but it was just taking time to get there. When Ron walked over, we talked about my long run and the pain I felt.

"You're just around the corner. Soon, this will just go away," he promised.

I realized I didn't need to come here anymore. I saw this knee problem as two pronged. First, I needed to know what my poor movements were and try to correct them. Second, I needed to build strength, which was coming along but was going to take time. I knew what I needed to do and was doing it.

"I think I'm going to start to work on this on my own," I

told Ron. He agreed and said to keep in touch and let him know if I had any further concerns.

Fixing my knee was my responsibility and I needed to take care of it. Leaving it up to someone else who sees me for only an hour every week was not miraculously going to work. I needed to learn from Ron, but then I needed to incorporate what he taught me about strengthening and my gait into my running plan. He wasn't there for my runs, he wasn't there for each step to tell me what I was doing wrong. I needed to monitor what worked and what made a step feel right or wrong and work on fixing that myself. I tried my best to stay focused, but the mental game of this whole project was huge. I didn't anticipate needing to think so much about so many different things. I thought running fifty miles would just be a physical challenge.

Up to that point, whenever I had a long run, I planned the number of miles I wanted to run and then I did it. When I finished, I couldn't imagine running farther than I just had—at fourteen, I couldn't see doing fifteen; at fifteen, I couldn't foresee doing sixteen; and so on. But then the next time I planned to go farther, I did it. I decided I needed to look at the miles on my training plan and see myself accomplishing what I want instead of comparing it to previous efforts. I couldn't be afraid of what I thought I couldn't do; my body had already come through with everything I'd asked it to do.

Even though I'd given myself a great pep talk about how my body had never failed, when a twenty-mile trail run appeared on the schedule, I was afraid. I'd told myself not to be, but I couldn't help it. There weren't any flat trails in my area and I couldn't come up with a route that didn't have some huge steep parts to it. My knee hurt after my first twenty-miler on roads; how would it not if I ran on trails?

I opened my laptop and composed an email to Ian. He clearly didn't understand that I could really hurt myself. "Are you sure I should do this on trail?"

When I got a response, worry plagued me. "You'll be fine. Power-hike the steep parts and go easy on the rest."

That sounded benign enough, but if I walked all the steep parts, I'd be walking about half of the run, and how long would that take? I was going to be out there for days! OK, not days, but a really long time. The twenty the previous week took me about three and a half hours. By my math, this trail run would take at least twice that.

* * *

Excerpt from the Becoming Ultra Podcast
Season 2 Episode 11
Tips to stay on track as an ultra runner around the holidays
December 18

Scott: Hey, welcome to Becoming Ultra, I'm your host Scott Jones. We have a fast show today, I'm sitting here at the rec center, my little four-year-old is about to sing some kind of Christmas carols. So, really quick, Ian, Janet, how are you guys doing?

Ian: So, Janet had her first twenty-miler last weekend, and we have another twenty miles on the trails tomorrow. Janet emailed me this week saying she's a little bit nervous about it. Her knee, which has been the constant theme and we've been trying to get past it, and that's not been acting perfectly, but we have been able to increase the mileage. So, how did it feel after last week's long run, Janet, and what are your thoughts going into tomorrow?

Janet: I think with the twenty-miler I have this idea that nothing is supposed to hurt. I need to change my thought pattern from, "this is a pain" to maybe "this is a soreness." Then watch it, and if in a couple of days, it heals up and it recovers, maybe it wasn't pain in the first place maybe it's just part of the process.

Ian: It's knowing the difference between a bit soreness, a bit of fatigue, it being tough, and something that's more like an injury. And that's something that obviously comes with experience, but this being your first marathon and fifty-miler, it's very difficult to know that.

Scott: And these are some things, for you guys listening, sharp pain, that's an issue. These more achy, hard to describe stiffness, while you're running, that's the threshold, that's the load that you're putting on to your body that will help you adapt. So, I'm about to go see my kid Christmas carol. Ian and Janet, thank you so much, I hope you guys have a great weekend, and a great Christmas.

CHAPTER 20

I set out the morning of the trail twenty-miler with a friend, Rachel. I explained to her that I'd be walking up the hills, and she agreed that would be fine. When we reached the seven-mile marker, she turned around and went back. I continued on to the beast, a steep part of the trail that seemed forgotten by the builders. Most sections like this had switchbacks, which made the climbs longer in distance, but easier in effort. This one hill was just straight up, and up, and up. I got to work on it, and it was all just hiking. In total, it was around three hundred feet. The mile that included that climb mile took me about fifteen minutes. Not too bad. I did a quick math calculation and at that pace, I'd be done in about five hours. After getting to the top, it was time to turn around and head back. I had to go down the steep section, which sounds easy enough, but it was so steep with loose gravel that I was just as slow going down as up.

Once I got to the bottom, I still had eight miles to go. I ran back easy and continued walking up anything steep. Near the end, I noticed that my knee wasn't hurting. That was a welcome surprise. Maybe it was the lack of pounding hard down that steep section. I noticed that the effort needed to go uphill forced me to use good form and my muscles had to do their job; they couldn't divert the effort to my joints. This was all coming together.

I finished in just over four hours! That was way less than I thought it would take. Add a 10K and take the hills out of it, and I might finish the marathon in a decent time. I was spent by the end of the run, and I was sore, but not in any kind of pain.

I got a text from Rachel saying, "That was way easier!" I think she'd been skeptical about the walking, too, fearing that it would take too long.

I got home and had to ascend a set of stairs, I lived in a second floor apartment. This is where the pain of my long runs tended to linger, I winced and carefully took the step. I was able to do it in proper form and without pain. Encouraged, I stood just a little taller. I ascended the rest and felt fine. True progress. I'm glad I didn't chicken out with the trail run. I was getting somewhere! For the rest of the day, I didn't feel so drained of energy. Maybe incorporating some walking, er, power hiking, was going to be beneficial.

On Christmas Day, I loaded my pack with water and some running gels. I didn't like the idea of using them, they didn't sound appetizing, but they were much more convenient than making my sweet potato mix. Ian told me to try different things in training, so by race day I knew what worked for me, and more importantly, what didn't. Then I charted a route around town and set out early for my first twenty-one-miler.

I got started running; the weather was cold but not uncomfortable. I saw a patch of ice on the pavement and jumped over it. I thought of last Christmas in Chicago and wondered if I would be running on ice-patched sidewalks, breathing supercooled air if I were back there this Christmas. I had enjoyed being home, but it just wasn't possible this year. Knowing that we weren't going home was one of the reasons I thought the Becoming Ultra project would be feasible. I wouldn't have the distraction of a trip in the middle of training, so it was easier to stay on track. Running this Christmas morning was proof of that.

I ran down a bike path that led to the far west end of town. When I reached the halfway point and turned around, I could see the mountain near my home in the distance. It never failed to amaze me how impressive it looked to be miles from home knowing that I did it on my own two feet. I took out a gel and squeezed the contents into my mouth. Yuck. It tasted awful, it felt gross, and it was sticky on my fingers. Sure, it was convenient, but what was the point if I didn't like it? I vowed to make more of my sweet potato mixes and look for other alternatives.

When I got to the last few miles, fatigue set in. My muscles were burning and my joints were screaming. I finished and leaned up against a tree to enjoy a moment standing still. I blocked the pain from my mind; I had another twenty-miler on the schedule next weekend. I considered where I wanted to run it. I'd seen an interesting New Year's Day run posted on Facebook called the Post-Apocalyptic Run. It was hosted by Natalia who organized the Tuesday runs. They were meeting early, about 6 a.m., on the Las Vegas strip and ran through the aftermath of New Year's Eve celebrations. Every year, Las Vegas shuts down the strip to car traffic and people are allowed to roam Las Vegas Boulevard. The casinos that participate put on an impressive coordinated fireworks display from the rooftops. When it's done, a cloud of smoke settles in over all the buildings and it looks like a war zone, or at least what I'd seen on TV of a war zone.

By 6 a.m., the street would be desolate. It sounded like an awesome time to roam the strip, but the group was only doing four miles and they would be stopping for pictures and in general enjoying the morning. I had to get twenty miles in. I didn't have time for goofing around. There was something else to consider: running on the strip meant running at least ten staircases leading to pedestrian walkways that stretched over the road. That was a lot of climbing and a lot of stress on my joints.

I pushed myself off of the tree I was leaning on and bent over to stretch the backs of my legs. Then I bent my knees to squat to the ground. It felt good, but when I got up it was difficult to walk. *How the heck was I going to run a marathon in a few weeks?* But if I was going to be in this much pain next week, too, I might as well enjoy the first four miles. I wouldn't think about the staircases just now; I was going to the Post-Apocalyptic Run.

CHAPTER 21

I arrived on the strip just before 6 a.m. on New Year's Day. I carpooled with two other runners who were also going and lived on my side of town. I planned to run home after the run, and didn't need to be going back to the strip to pick up a car. The sun wasn't up yet, and the strip was mostly deserted. Temporary fences were still in place on Las Vegas Boulevard. I met up with the run group on the north end of the strip. I had met most of the people in the group already. We said our hellos and started running.

We ran to the south on the east side of the strip. Within the first quarter mile, we reached the first staircase and I walked it, trying to be gentle. We passed a girl who was underdressed for the temperature, her hair was a mess, and her sparkly heels, the height of which made my calves cringe, dangled from her hands. She was walking barefoot. Looked like she'd had quite a night. We ran down the staircase and then passed the deep blue watered canals of Italy at the Venetian.

We ran past several groups of young millennials who were still inebriated and dressed in tight suits. Each group was astonished that we could possibly be running at this hour. They cheered, gave us high fives, and a few even tried to run with us —for about ten feet. After several more staircases, we got to Tropicana Avenue and stopped in front of the MGM. We took some selfies in front of the giant golden lions as we breathed through invisible clouds of marijuana odor. I laughed and so did everyone else. At this point, having covered about two miles, we turned around and headed back, which required traversing three sets of staircases to start going north on the west side of the street. Up from the MGM and down to the Tropicana. Then up and down to the Excalibur. Then up and down to the New York New York. My knee felt fine, but I still walked up and down all of these to minimize any negative effects. Once on the west side, we passed through the new Brooklyn Bridge of New York New York. We passed the new Central Park that was still under construction and fenced off. We passed the Bellagio and the still pool of the fountains in front. The sun was coming up, and as it began to stream rays of light between the buildings on the east side of the street, it cast shadows that danced through the trees lining the thoroughfare in front of the fountains. In front of Caesar's Palace, we stopped at a Buddhist shrine that I'd never seen before. We lit incense sticks that were provided. The strip was filled with little gems like this. After about an hour, we returned to the start.

Everyone was getting coffee, but I had more miles to go. I ate a rice cake that I prepared; something new I was trying from the Feed Zone Portables cookbook. The rice was combined with an apple, sugar, salt, and cinnamon and according to the cookbook, was a good source of energy to take while I was running. I then said my goodbyes and set out to run home, which I estimated was about sixteen miles away—perfect. I passed McCarran Airport and ate some gummy candies. I ran through some neighborhoods on the south end of Las Vegas Boulevard and ate a Honey Stinger waffle cookie. I got to the bike path along the highway and had to stop to address a growing blister on my foot. I had bandages, so I made a quick patch and got back at it. After a few more neighborhoods, I got to the Pittman Wash bike path. My knee was starting to speak up, and I tried to ignore it. I downed a Skratch Labs electrolyte drink and continued. I was about six miles from home.

After a few more miles, I couldn't ignore my knee anymore. It hurt and I regretted my decision to include all of those stairs. *Why did I do that?* Because I wanted to have fun—I needed to remember that. This pain wouldn't last forever, and I wanted this training to be more than just prepping my body. I wanted to be able to look back on this training and have some good memories to think about. This was my last long run before my first-ever marathon, so I had to finish it. I needed to learn how to cope with the pain when I had no intention of quitting. I concentrated my energies on very small increments of time. When I passed a tree, I thought about how cool looking that particular tree was. I thought about the intricate details of how it looked, its bark and its leaves. Then I got out my cranberries and focused solely on eating some of them. A person approached with a terrier in tow. I looked at that dog and observed how happy he looked, trotting along with his tongue out. In keeping my mind occupied on one singular thing, I found that I forgot about my knee long enough to get through another half mile or so. I stopped a few times and stretched out my legs, then bent them up to my chest, one at a time. That felt good. Then I continued.

When my watch finally ticked the last mile and I was just about home, I sat down and gave my knee a break. I was at the top of a hill, and I looked out at the Las Vegas valley. Anytime you get a view of the valley, you can see the strip—from the Luxor pyramid at the far south to the Stratosphere at the far north. I smiled realizing that whenever I saw that landmark now, I could remember that I ran home from there. I felt proud and didn't care about my knee at that moment.

When I got home, I logged my run and sent my physical therapist a message. I explained my recent runs and the continued knee pain. He explained that I was doing much better than I was just a few months ago and that the increased mileage was definitely a factor in the continued pain; it would take time for the connective tissue of my knee to adapt. He said my recovery was still heading in the right direction and not to worry.

I also sent Ian an email about how it went. I was frustrated with my knee but felt I'd done it to myself with all those stairs.

Ian was not as concerned as I thought he would be. He reminded me that I had asked a lot of my body and told me not to worry —I had two weeks until the marathon. A few days after the New Year's Day run, my knee felt better.

* * *

Excerpt from the Becoming Ultra Podcast
Season 2 Episode 13
Her first marathon is a training run
January 8

Scott: Hey welcome to the Becoming Ultra show, I am Scott Jones, your host. Janet is coming up on a marathon soon, and we've been following her journey to run the American River 50 in April. So, how's the training going?

Ian: So obviously this is a difficult time of year for people to keep their routine, when you have Thanksgiving, then Christmas, then the New Year, it's not the normal work schedule, the normal running schedule, plus the weather for many people, although not if you live in the Vegas area, tends to be a little bit more difficult, too.

Janet: I had it pretty easy this year because I didn't go home for the holidays. The biggest thing is that its dark and its cold and everybody's doing different things and so you don't have your normal people to run with. It's been really helpful to have a training schedule; I don't wake up and say "it's kinda cold out, I don't want to do it," nope, today I'm doing this.

Ian: Whenever Janet has any questions, or we need to adjust anything we do that and we work out how to maximize the time that she has available. The main thing in keeping that consistency is the lingering problem we've had from the very beginning which is her knee, which has been improving the whole time, and now it gets much later into runs before it's a problem. We've identified which things make it flare up a little bit more, and that tends to be the downhills, so we've been careful with that, and having the corrective exercises to strengthen the legs and the stabilization muscles, as well as getting just more fitness from the regular running and gradual increase of mileage.

But basing that increase on how her body is responding to the training. We've had some longer runs, we've done over twenty miles a couple of times, so that sets her up really nicely for doing a road marathon.

Janet: It's just really hard when I get done with a twenty-miler and I still have six more miles.

Ian: The simplest way to give you confidence is that it just kind of works. It's weird, but the body is incredibly good at adapting. You'll realize that even with some low points, and very likely going through a wall at around the twenty mile mark, you'll realize just what's possible and that you can come through the other side. It's not that you hit a wall and you're screwed, it's that you hit a wall, you deal with things, but then you keep going. It's almost like an epiphany the first time that happens to you.

Scott: It's very rare that someone uses their first marathon as a training run. How would you like to speak to the mentality of all that.

Ian: So much about ultra running is about your mental toughness. We've turned the marathon into a step to the ultra, so it's really about outlook.

Scott: Most people have more left in the tank when they're stopping something.

Ian: You usually can do more than you expect.

Scott: Good Luck, Janet. Thanks so much for joining me. Janet's a trooper and she's doing great with her training.

CHAPTER 22

After my New Year's Day twenty-mile run home from the Las Vegas strip, I settled in to enjoying the taper—that time between my last long run and the marathon. It's like money in the bank: I'd already done all the work. I had no new injuries so now I just had to wait and run the marathon.

I tried to calm my nerves and focus on preparing. I posted on the Becoming Ultra page, asking for advice—I wanted to know what others had kept in mind for their first marathon. I got some good tips: Trim your toenails about a week ahead. Go to the bathroom before the race and then go again. Think of the twenty-mile mark as the halfway. That was a really good one. At thirteen miles, I would still be feeling pretty good; it was a mile marker I'd grown used to and wouldn't be the halfway of my effort. The twenty-mile point would be a much better distance for me to evaluate the effort I'd put in and the likely effort I could proceed with.

Krystal was progressing well in her training, too. She had decided to fly out and run the marathon, too. I was glad she was coming; she was much more experienced than I and hopefully she could help calm my nerves.

The week before the marathon, I prepped my sweet potato mix and some oatmeal. Dan and I were travelling to California on Friday to stay with some friends in Huntington Beach, about an hour north of the race location in Carlsbad. I didn't want to rely on having the time to prep my foods at their house; I hoped it would still be good on Sunday. I packed several potential outfits for the race. I wasn't sure if I would want to wear shorts, or capris; a t-shirt or a long sleeved shirt. After getting all my race items packed, I packed regular clothes for a few days. I had more luggage than I take on an airplane.

Dan and I got to our friends' house, and we enjoyed some time with them. We went out to a Mexican place to eat, and I tried to order something without any spice. But Mexican food is my favorite, and so many other things looked tempting. Dan and our friends enjoyed some drinks, I did not. I didn't want to chance feeling queasy from alcohol. We hung out at a café on the beach, and took a long walk to get there. *What if my legs got tired from this?* I tried to hide my anxiety. Maybe I would enjoy a destination race in the future, but so far, it just made everything more complicated.

On Saturday, I drove to Carlsbad and met Krystal at the race expo. We ran into Alison while we were there. She was a listener of the Becoming Ultra podcasts, she lived in the area, and was running the marathon, too. We made plans to meet up in the morning at the race start. Krystal and I left and got to the hotel room. We chatted and got to know each other. She asked if I wanted her to pace me, I said no. With her pace being so much faster than mine, she would feel like she was walking at my pace. The last thing I needed was to be worrying about whether or not someone else was enjoying themselves or not. Good thing, too, because her plan for this race was to run fast enough to qualify for entry into the Boston Marathon.

At the time, the two weeks prior to the marathon took forever, but looking back, they flew by. I was anxious and excited all at the same time. I was going to be a marathoner; I wasn't sure how long that was going to take, but I was going to cross that finish line. I'd put in so much work and effort, and I could see me with that medal around my neck. So many people have accomplished a marathon, and now I would be a marathoner, too.

Scott wanted to tape a podcast, so we set up for that. It was an even-numbered week, so it was Krystal and Liza's episode. But since we were together, I would join in.

* * *

Excerpt from Season 2 Episode 14
The Carlsbad Marathon Weekend. One marathon, two reasons
January 16

Scott: Hey everybody, welcome to the Becoming Ultra show. We're doing something a little different this week. We have Krystal and Janet in the same room. Liza's joining us today and Janet's about to run her first marathon tomorrow. Janet, how are you feeling today? Not many people use their first marathon as a training run.

Janet: I'm nervous, it's a lot longer than I've run, but it's kind of overshadowed with, just that I've thought about it for so long, I'm ready to run it and have it done. And this is a destination marathon, so there's been a lot of packing and not having food available that I'm used to. I'm just ready to get to the start line and do this.

Scott: And Krystal, how about you?

Krystal: I'm happy to be here, happy to support Janet, I'm so glad we were able to meet, and I'm excited for tomorrow. We met at the expo. We're ready to get our stuff out and get ready for tomorrow.

Scott: What did you do today, how are you gonna prep tonight, what's the game plan?

Janet: Well, again, because it's out of town, nothing is going as I'm used to doing it. Earlier today, I was hanging out with some friends at the beach, and we went for a really long walk. So, we'll see if that was a good idea.

Liza: Oh no! (Laughing) Rookie mistake.

Janet: I had to bring all my foods that I prepped on Thursday, so hopefully that's still good. That's what I plan to eat during the race.

Scott: Liza, why don't you chime in. What do you think Janet needs to focus on?

Liza: I think that, for a lot of folks it's hard to sleep before the first marathon. Just don't stress about that. A bad night's sleep before this race is not gonna affect it. Just get everything prepared, get your clothes all ready so in the morning you don't have to do much thinking, and you just want to set yourself up for as little stress as possible. But then, you're just gonna have a fine time tomorrow. You're gonna do 26.2 miles, and you're gonna learn a lot of stuff, and it's your first one, so there's no pressure to run faster than your last one. Just enjoy it.

Scott: I liked on the Facebook page for Becoming Ultra, Janet wanted some tips for her first marathon, and their advice was: thirteen is not the halfway point. Twenty is the halfway point. Does that help you mentally?

Janet: Yes. I'm looking at this as a 10K race with a twenty mile warm up.

Scott: So Krystal, you're going for a BQ here, a Boston Qualifier, right?

Krystal: My heart just skipped a beat. Yes!

Scott: What's the qualifier for you?

Krystal: 3:35.

Scott: Krystal, Janet, good luck tomorrow. Thanks a lot for listening you guys.

CHAPTER 23

On the morning of the marathon, I woke before my alarm; my mind was racing too much to sleep. I was ready to start this thing. I'd spent so much time thinking about the marathon; now I just wanted to do it.

I got out of bed and started getting ready. Krystal turned on some fast-paced, get-you-in-the-mood music as she got ready. I needed to have my oatmeal at least an hour before race start. There was a microwave in the lobby, but I didn't want to waste time with that, so I ate it cold—not something I suggest. Krystal and I had two different goals for today: I wanted to finish this thing and feel good about the experience. Based on my training, I thought I should finish around 4:30, but I really wanted 4:20, which would be a ten-minute-mile pace. Krystal wanted to qualify for Boston, which meant she had to get around 3:30. Wowsers.

After donning all of my gear, I took out my huge, fluffy pink bathrobe and threw it around me, tossing the hood over my head. Krystal laughed, and I smiled. I gave a little one-two jab like Rocky; time to get on with this.

We checked out of the hotel and took the shuttle to the race staging tent. Krystal messaged Alison, who met up with us. I took off the pink bathrobe and stuffed it in my bag, which I left in the drop area. It was still dark out, and the air was cool and damp. I was feeling good and I lifted my legs a few times to loosen them up. We got to the start line, snapped a few selfies, and then Krystal headed up to the front where the competitors were. Alison said she planned a 4:45, so I hung with her. The race started and I was off, finally running a marathon.

I felt really good, but I knew this was a game of pacing, so I stuck with Alison. She had run many marathons, so I relied on her experience to set the pace. We were doing a ten-minute-mile pace, but it felt slow—oh, so slow. So I concentrated on other things. We ran through the town of Carlsbad, which was still asleep; the stores hadn't opened yet. It was a quaint town that I could see myself enjoying by having breakfast in one of the cafes or relaxing with a beer in one of the bars.

About half of the course was on a road up a cliff overlooking the ocean. There were surfers paddling among the waves, enjoying a high surf advisory. After a few miles, I noticed a small pack of runners, one of which was holding a stick in the air that read: 4:30. This was one of the pacer groups. They were going a little fast, but their strategy was to run ten-minute miles and slow down after twenty. Perfect. That's when the great unknown would happen for me. What would miles twenty-one to twenty-six be like? I settled in with the group. These girls were incredible. They had us running near-perfect ten-minute miles and reminded us to eat every half hour or so.

Alison and I had just met so we talked about life and kids —well, her kids—and jobs. We talked running and mileages. She told me she'd run the American River 50 before, so I asked her any question that popped in my head about what that was like. Was it all trail? Were there hills? Should I wear trail shoes, or road shoes, or swap them out at the halfway point? How did it work with pacers? Was I going to die?

Somewhere around mile nine, after climbing a large hill, I stuck with the pacer group and Alison fell behind. I couldn't let them get out of my sight, or I would never catch up. I was thankful Alison had run with me this far; without her, the excitement of the race would have made me run too fast at the beginning.

Around mile twelve the course turned perpendicular to

the ocean, so I was running toward the Pacific Ocean. The beauty was striking, with the waves crashing in and the blue skies above. I pressed my chest out, and a wave of emotion washed over me. I choked back tears. I was doing it! I was running a marathon! How many years had I wanted to do this but never put the work in to get there? How often had I convinced myself that it wasn't important just because I didn't want to commit to the goal? How often did I think my knee would never make it, so why even try? If I was this emotional now, what the heck was gonna happen when I crossed the finish line? I shook my head and blinked my eyes and reminded myself that I hadn't done it yet; I still had a lot of work in front of me.

Around mile fourteen came my first ache—my lower back. It was a reminder to adjust my posture. A guy in a multicolored jester wig was running next to me and holding a cow bell—clank, clank, clank. *Ugh, that is annoying!* Then Krystal's voice rang in my head: "Nothing negative." I'm more of a cynic and not nearly as upbeat as her, so I decided to trust in Krystal's experience in this area. I pushed back the idea that the bell was annoying and reframed it in a positive way: the bell clanked with every step and the guy had a good cadence going, so I used it to keep mine in check.

Between miles fifteen and twenty, I had a myriad of aches and pains. A pain on my foot hurt for a while. When it started, I thought, *Here we go. This pain is going to get worse and worse until I can't take it anymore.* However, after a mile or so, it went away. After that, another pain started in my knee, and again I thought, *Here we go. I'm going to have to stop.* It also went away after a few miles. A new pain started in my left hip. *What is that about?* I had to get my mind around this whole feat: I was asking a lot of my body and it was fighting back. I had to trust in the training and know that I was prepared for this.

At mile twenty, the 4:30 pacer group I was running with started to slow down. The girl holding the stick yelled, "You in the teal. How do you feel?"

I looked down to see my shirt and realized that was me.

I assessed my feelings: nothing was painful, and nothing ached too bad. I felt like this could go on for some time. "I feel great!"

"Keep going!" the pacer said.

So I did. Miles twenty-one and twenty-two still felt great and I maintained the ten-minute-mile pace, but I had signs of mental fatigue. Spectators lined most of the course and offered encouragement, and since my name was written on my bib, they cheered me by name. That was awesome—until about mile twenty-two. A group cheered, "You can do it, Janet!" I snarled and hoped they couldn't see it. *I know I can, but it's taking forever.* I had to get the attitude in check. These people took time out of their day to cheer on their loved ones, but they also cheered for me. My mind was messing with me.

Then mile twenty-three came. I've heard of the wall and I was respectfully afraid of it. I had eaten every half hour since the first hour and had taken an electrolyte drink at about 2.5 hours and a salt tab around 3 hours. I wasn't cramping so I was still able to move my legs, but it was as if my body was trying to take over my mind and just make me stop. I had to concentrate on every single step. I felt the motion of every part of those strides. My left foot pushing off, my right leg pulling forward, my right foot hitting the ground, my left leg pulling forward, my left foot striking the ground. One foot in front of the other. When my feet were in the air, they were momentarily happy, but then inevitably I landed on one and it ached with disapproval. I think my feet were just tired of being stepped on at that point. I wasn't giving myself a choice to stop, so this was how I was going to spend the next hour. One foot in front of the other. I just kept repeating that in my head. One foot in front of the other.

I hadn't planned to run the entire race without walking a few times, but it became clear that the 4:20 goal wasn't going to happen, so I wanted a new goal to focus on. I'd made it this far without stopping. I'd run through every aid station because I was fully equipped with my own pack, so my new goal was to run the whole thing; this would be a big mental accomplishment. I repeated, one foot in front of the other. A large costumed person stood in the middle of the road; he was green and had a long snout. I tried to think of what he was from—a mascot for a company? A character from a movie? It never clicked, but he put up his big furry paw and I gave him a high five. A half mile went by before I thought about my steps again, and then the monotony returned. One foot in front of the other. I was looking down at the ground and sweat dripped from my visor one drop at a time. I looked up. A man stood in the middle of the road with a microphone and rapped a song. Earlier in the race, the entertainment was on the sides of the road; now they stood where you couldn't avoid them. I was glad for the more interactive experience. I high-fived him, too. It momentarily got my mind off my steps. Another half mile went by, and the thought of each step returned. This is how the final miles passed, but I didn't walk a single one. One foot in front of the other.

As I approached the finish line, the 4:30 pacer appeared out of nowhere. "Come on girl, you can do it!" she yelled.

I looked at the time. I was gonna break 4:30. I sped up my steps into an all-out sprint. I'm sure it looked ridiculous for the spectators, as though I was trying to say that's how fast I'd run the whole thing, which at four and a half hours, clearly I had not. But it felt good to get my legs moving more, and you know, goals. I crossed the finish line with the pacer right next to me just under 4:30. It felt good, but my body was spent. I walked through the shoot collecting my medal, a large piece of silver foil, a brown paper bag with some foods, and a chocolate milk. It took every ounce of my brain power to walk and manage all of the items I'd just acquired. Krystal found me at the finish line, she'd finished an hour earlier. She got her BQ! We, well mostly me, waddled away from the race.

There wasn't anything left in me to be the bawling mess of pride that I'd feared at mile twelve. That was OK. It felt good to be physically and mentally spent, and I'd done it. I was now a marathoner.

CHAPTER 24

The next few days were awesome. I posted on Becoming Ultra's Facebook page about my marathon finish. I posted on my own page, too, and the congratulations and likes came pouring in. I checked my page every few minutes and saw more and more comments. I let my phone sit for a while so that when I checked it again, there were numerous notifications. It was a real ego boost that anyone cared that I'd done this. People said I was inspiring, which was weird for me, but I thanked them anyway. I hadn't done anything extraordinary —millions of other people have also run a marathon—but this was my time, my moment. I also knew that this was the only first marathon I would ever run, so I enjoyed all the attention.

My mom called me and told me how proud she was. It's odd in my forties to have my mom be proud of me. For something totally unnecessary. I hadn't helped anyone; I hadn't built anything important or saved anyone. I just put my mind to something and followed through. Was that worthy of pride? I could tell in her voice that she was disappointed she hadn't been there. "I'll be at the fifty-miler," she vowed.

The overwhelming sense of achievement I thought I would have at the finish line hadn't happened; instead it came slowly over the next few days as I realized the monkey on my back was gone. I felt really accomplished, proud of myself for setting a goal and sticking with it.

After the marathon I went on a four-day running hiatus. I enjoyed that time. I ate whatever I wanted and didn't think about calories or sugar content. I went to Coldstone Creamery and got a huge waffle cup with a scoop of chocolate ice cream mixed with brownies and caramel. I enjoyed every last bite of it.

I barely had time to relax and settle in as a marathoner before turning my thoughts to the ultra. I was disappointed that this next challenge overshadowed my moment as a marathoner, but that was OK. It was time to focus on the American River 50.

Over the previous three months since I agreed to the ultra run, I often felt overwhelmed by what Ian asked me to do. Being an ultra runner was outlandish, and taking the steps to reach that goal was tough to reconcile. I kept these feelings in check by reminding myself that those steps had prepared me for the marathon; I would have been doing that training anyway. In fact, if I had been on my own, I would have stuck to an online training program and not allowed it to fluctuate based on my knee issues. I wouldn't have gone to a physical therapist; I just wouldn't have. So the truth was Ian and Scott got me to the marathon in way better shape than I would have been through a self-directed training program. I may or may not have been able to run it on my own, but it surely would have hurt much worse. The process would have been filled with fear and doubts.

Nevertheless, how the heck could I run fifty miles? I thought about not going further in this journey, of stopping at my marathon goal. As I'd seen throughout the training, when I completed the marathon, I couldn't imagine running another step, and it was impossible to think of almost doubling that distance. I thought about my marathon goal and how I'd been thinking about doing a marathon ever since I was a kid running all those road races that my mom took me to. I harbored that goal my whole life, and it only took a few months of commitment to do it. Why did I wait so long? What else was I putting off thinking it would be too difficult or that I'll get to it one day? Maybe there were other things that were also just a short time away if I just dedicated myself to it and focused on it. The fifty-miler was one of these challenges. I'd already done so much work for it, there was no way I was quitting. I owed Scott and Ian this journey, and I also wanted to see if I could do it. I had only two and a half months of training left; I could do that.

I opened my training plan and looked past the marathon. What would training for an ultra look like? Ian had put my first back-to-back weekend on the schedule. Eighteen miles on a Friday and eighteen miles on a Saturday. Well, that just got real.

* * *

Excerpt from the Becoming Ultra Podcast
Season 2 Episode 15
Glad we got that little marathon out of the way
January 22

Scott: Hey welcome to the Becoming Ultra show. I'm hanging out with Ian and Janet. We're following Janet's journey, and all things ultra running. Ian, Janet, how are you guys doing today? Janet, tell us about the marathon.

Janet: The marathon turned out to be a really good experience for me. Krystal flew all the way across the country so she could run it too, and that was amazing because she's experienced at this so she knew things to tell me like bring flip flops or what time should we get to the marathon, things I didn't need to worry about and I could just focus on the race. She, the day before, asked if I wanted her to pace me, and I said, you run way too fast, you're gonna feel like you're walking, so I said no. Turned out to be fine because Alison, one of our followers, she ran the first nine miles with me. As for the race itself, miles one to twenty, I felt great. Twenty to twenty-two, I still felt good, I was just adjusting to what my body was telling me. Miles twenty-three to twenty-six, that's when it got tough, it wasn't anything specific, it was a mental challenge at that point to say am I gonna finish this thing or not. I finished just under 4:30 which is where I thought I should be, and I couldn't have been happier. It was just a really good run.

Ian: Especially for your first one, to have it go well. There's so much that can go wrong, the first time that you do a distance, there's such a learning curve to it. The knee still wasn't perfect going into it, and the fact that it wasn't an issue, I think that is a massive success, and also a huge confidence boost. The good thing is, if you have the marathon fitness, you kind of have the fifty-mile fitness, it's not a huge leap. You'll want to use some power hiking in the ultra. In ultras, slowing down a little bit doesn't have a huge effect on your time, so throwing in hiking breaks, spending a couple of minutes at the aid station, doesn't have much effect when the finish time is so much longer. It's partly that mentality of just knowing that the whole thing will be a bit more slower, a little bit more relaxed, and that you've got the fitness already to be able to get through that, it's just making that effort level last a little bit longer, by having hiking breaks, by eating more, and things that we'll focus on over the coming couple of months with your long runs.

Scott: Has the hiking been introduced yet?

Ian: We've had some, but it will become a bigger and bigger part of it. Especially in the long runs, to keep the intensity just a bit lower. It's about being efficient to finish an ultra, not about being fast. So, if we improve her top speed, that's gonna help Janet, but if we can improve her minimum speed, that speed she's going at even if she feels really bad, that's gonna have a much bigger effect. Let's say the top speed goes up by a minute a mile, she saves one minute in a mile. If the bottom speed goes up from being a forty minute death march, to a fifteen minute strong power hike, and that's the minimum, then she can save twenty-five minutes in one single mile.

Scott: So now, what is the training gonna look like?

Ian: One of the key things is that we'll be doing more trails. It'll be more focused on mimicking the specifics of the race that we're training for. Second, we're gonna throw in some back-to-back long runs. We'll probably have two or three of these. The first one is a few weeks away. It's eighteen miles on a Friday and Saturday. So a really big training weekend, but neither of the days are super long. So the benefit of doing a back-to-back is that it's a little bit easier on the body, you can keep up a higher quality within it, because if you're trying to do thirty-six miles all in one go, there's gonna be more slow down, while if we have it as two separate days there's a much better chance of still being able to run well on both days. And the other thing is a much quicker recovery.

Scott: So we're working on structural adaptation and intermuscular and what's going on in her joints and being able to handle the wear and tear but with quality long runs so that she's building confidence along the way. Do you have a goal for the longest run before the event?

Ian: At this point, it depends. I would say the longest run we're likely to do is about thirty or thirty-one miles, so around a 50K, about a month out from the ultra.

Janet: It's almost amazing to see where I was three months ago to where I am today. Just the muscles that are different and my capabilities, and we still have two and a half months. What's gonna be different between me now and then?

Ian: I think that's important for those listening to see what is possible in just a short amount of time. The body is just so good at adapting.

Scott: Stress plus rest equals adaptation.

Janet: I have one question, on one of our very first podcasts we were guessing what my time would be. Ian said he wanted to wait until after the marathon. So what's my time gonna be?

Ian: That's a tough one. I would say we are looking sub ten.

Janet: Wow.

Scott: I appreciate you guys as always. Thanks a lot.

CHAPTER 25

During the podcast, Ian stressed the importance of learning power hiking as a strategy for efficiency. I had already noticed that when I used hiking in my longer trail runs, it didn't really affect my pace significantly and left me with more energy at the end of a run. I was encouraged to hear that this would be part of my strategy. I was so much more fit now than I was three months ago when I started this training. I looked forward to seeing what a few more months would bring.

My first trail run after the marathon was an eight-miler about a week later. The ultra was on trails, so the rest of my training would focus on that. Cheyenne from Run Grrrls Run organized a group run out at Cottonwood Valley on the west side. We met on a chilly morning; the surrounding mountains were snowcapped, the sky was overcast, and a morning blue hue cast a peaceful aura over the area. I couldn't have been happier. I loved being on the trails and wanted to run them more. Goosebumps sprouted up my arms as the group gathered, so I hopped in place to get my blood moving. We set out on the same route as the half marathon trail race I'd run in November. The peace and quiet of the open desert made me feel at home.

I warmed up after a half mile or so and enjoyed the decline of the first few miles. I'd done a test run earlier in the week and felt fine. Now, after a few miles, my left hip started to hurt again like it did in the marathon. I tried to convince myself that it wasn't getting worse, but it felt just as painful—a deep and dull but persistent and present pain with every step. It was the same leg as my knee pain, I wondered if they were a related issue? I decided to make an appointment with my physical therapist. I hadn't seen him since well before the marathon. It wouldn't hurt to have a checkup and see what he thought. I had more than two months of training left, and any advice I could get to make those injury free would be welcomed.

After I got home and got something to eat, I opened my laptop to check my schedule. I had a sixteen-mile trail run for the upcoming weekend. I nodded my head with confidence. Three months ago, I would have been anxious about that distance, wondering if it was too much and how would I feel at the end. Now, sixteen trail miles were much easier to wrap my brain around. It was a distance far below my maximum, and the thought of running on trails and being out in the desert exploring sounded like a great day to me. I pulled up some maps and started to think about where to go.

An alert from a Facebook group popped up on my computer. I clicked on it and a group event opened: a ten-mile run at Cowboy Trails. My eyebrows perked; I hadn't run that area before. I did some research and found numerous trails on the west end of the valley near a horse ranch. I looked at a map with topography and saw that many of these were steep. My expression fell; I couldn't do that. I needed to make sure I could run the miles, not kill myself on steep climbs. I sat back in my chair and crossed my arms. I wanted to check out the new trails, and it would be better doing that with someone who knew them. I didn't want to do all of this training having just rerun all the same stuff I already knew. I leaned forward and clicked the "Going" button next to the event.

Then I checked my email. Ian had sent a message. "You should pick out a thirty-mile trail race."

Thirty miles? On a trail? I know Ian said I would be ready, but how the heck was I going to do that? *I wish I could stop asking myself that question.* I double checked my training schedule. He hadn't written the thirty-miler in yet; I breathed a sigh of relief.

I searched the Desert Dash website. The Blood, Sweat, and Beers race took place at the end of February, which would be perfect timing, just about a month from the American River 50. I clicked on the race website. There was a marathon distance, so I could run that and add four miles to get thirty, but the race was in Bootleg Canyon—the trail system where I'd bit the dust on Labor Day. It was steep and rocky, and I'd stayed away from it for the most part. The marathon had over three thousand feet of elevation gain. That was too much, right? I looked for other races, but there weren't any in the valley. I looked to Arizona and found a really cool looking race called Antelope Canyon. The pictures of the race course were beautiful, but the reviews talked about a tough course with sand in a lot of areas. I wanted to get in a long run, not take on another challenge. I looked to Utah and found the Red Mountain 50K. That race looked scenic, but it also had a lot of elevation. I rolled my eyes. Why couldn't any of this be easy? I emailed Ian, "Are you sure I can do thirty miles with three thousand feet of gain?" He replied, "Yes, that one would be good." Ugh.

I woke up early on the morning of the Cowboy Trails group run. The group was only doing ten, so I stopped in nearby Blue Diamond first and set out for six miles. Ian talked about time on feet being an important factor more than just how many consecutive miles were run, so I didn't worry about breaking these miles into two separate runs of six and ten. The air was cold and peaceful and my run was easy. I didn't notice my hip hurting. Maybe it healed itself. My physical therapy session was in a few days so I would hopefully get some insight.

After my six, I drove to location number two. A small group of girls was gathered. I recognized a few faces from the Facebook page, but I hadn't met any of them before. I didn't mention that I'd already run six miles; I didn't want them thinking I would be a hindrance to the group or wouldn't be able to go the distance. However, on these group trail runs, no one seemed to care what your pace was. The groups I had run with were usually more than happy to let everyone run at their own pace, and then everyone waited now and then to make sure no one got lost. It was pretty easy going and stress free.

We ran straight up a steep trail, so I power-hiked the first part. I met Beth who talked about how she'd run the American River 50 before, and she planned to do it again this year. I asked her all the questions I could think of. We discussed the thirty-miler I needed to plan, and I mentioned the Blood, Sweat, and Beers race. I was hoping she would agree with me, that it would be too difficult. She didn't; in fact, she said she was running it for her training, too. Ugh. These ultra folks were beasts.

We then traversed some more moderate sections. About half way through, we got up to the top of a ridge and I stood at the edge of a steep drop off. I'd seen this ridge from my home at the other end of the valley. It was so cool to be standing on it. I looked across the valley and saw all of Las Vegas, the strip, and Henderson in the distance. It was impressive and relaxing. We took pictures, attempting some where we jumped in the air and appeared to hover in space, weightless. It was fun to jump around on the top of a plateau. Then we started the descent. The trail took us down an incredibly steep section with lots of loose rocks, and I traversed with care. The decline on one mile was 675 feet! I was surprised that my knee wasn't spiking in pain and that my muscles were supporting my steps. Maybe I was getting stronger.

After we reached the bottom and the trail flattened out, I returned to my normal pace easily and nothing hurt. *Maybe I am ready for difficult trails*, I mused. *Maybe I can run my thirty miles on a tough course.* And that was that—I decided to run the Blood, Sweat, and Beers trail marathon, with a four-mile warm-up.

The official marathon photos had been posted on the website, and I took a look at them. It was cool to see me running, in a marathon! I couldn't believe I finally did it. I looked at Krystal's pictures, too. One in particular epitomized her skill as a runner. She looked so confident and strong, and the look on her face said, "Did this thing even start yet?" I laughed and sent Krystal the pic and my quote. I looked back at my set of pictures and cringed when I saw one where I was on my left leg, the bad knee leg. My whole torso dipped down when my left leg hit the ground. I couldn't prevent that from happening; my leg just wasn't strong enough yet. This was an eye-opening moment. I could see what was wrong, but until I was strong enough, there was only so much my body could do. My PT appointment was still a day away. I headed to the gym to work on my strength training. I was only doing one day a week, and I had a routine that took me about thirty to forty minutes to complete. I took this time seriously because I'd seen the benefits I was getting. Now seeing that I still had a long way to go, I worked even harder.

I tried to replicate the exercises my physical therapist had shown me. He had me use ankle weights and do hip and glute exercises from a lying down position. I didn't have ankle weights at my gym, so I chose a standup weight machine to work on those muscles. I then proceeded to the weight bar and did squats with weights. I was up to 125 pounds, but I realized that I wasn't getting the range of motion with such a heavy weight. So I pulled the weight back significantly and used just the bar, which was thirty-five pounds. I made sure to squat as close to the ground as I could. I did a set of ten, and then put a ten-pound weight on each end and did another set of ten with fifty-five pounds, making sure to get deep into the motion. Then I added five pounds to each side and did three sets of six with sixty-five pounds.

I then proceeded to box jumps—not my favorite, but I was getting better at them. I noticed that my left knee was swinging out just before I jumped, so I set up in front of a mirror to make sure I kept proper form. Knee over foot. I was getting better at landing softly, too.

I lifted some hand weights to keep my arms in shape. I did lunges with a fifteen-pound weight ball lifted over my head. I did planks, too. Well, one plank, for about a minute.

The next day, my hip hurt again and I didn't even run. Thankfully, my PT visit was that day. When I arrived, Ron congratulated me on the marathon. I smiled; I'd missed the attention. I thanked him because without his help, I wouldn't have gotten through it without my knee being a problem.

We discussed how the race went, and I told him how my hip started hurting in the race and had nagged me ever since. I thought it was getting better, but then the pain returned. I told him about my routine at the gym. I told him I was working hard, but smart. I showed him how I had adapted his exercises to what I had available in my gym.

He watched what I was doing, and then said, "That's it. That's why you're having pain there. You're doing the hip exercise wrong."

CHAPTER 26

"You've got to be kidding me," I stopped the exercise and drooped my shoulders.

Ron showed me the difference: during the lying-down exercise, I was on my left side, legs stacked with an ankle weight on my right leg. I lifted my right leg into the air then lowered it behind my left leg, I could feel my glute engaging. When I tried to replicate this in my gym with the machine, I was standing instead of lying down. I stood on my left leg and then swung my right leg back and forth in front of my left. This was putting stress on my hip, I could feel the difference. It was such a simple thing and I was screwing it up in such a major way. I was glad that it would be an easy fix, but it scared me to think of how easy it was to get some of this stuff wrong. I was thankful I'd gone to a physical therapist in the first place and definitely glad I'd gone back for a checkup.

I left the office and went back home. I opened my laptop and reviewed my training plan. My first back-to-back was that weekend: eighteen miles on Friday and eighteen miles on Saturday. I was fortunate to work four 10-hour shifts so I had Fridays off. My expression and shoulders tensed. One eighteen-mile run was not a difficult thing at this point; I'd been running twenty miles on a regular basis before the marathon. Doing it two days in row? That was incomprehensible.

I sat back in my chair and stared blankly at the computer.

My joints hurt at the end of long runs and I spent the following day relaxing; how the heck would I be able to wake up and run? I took a deep breath and decided I couldn't worry about that. Back-to-back runs were the heart of the ultra training. Ian said that I could get the endurance benefits from the miles without the stress of one extremely long run and the recovery time required afterward. In breaking it up over two days, I gave my body time to recoup.

I felt myself becoming anxious thinking about these runs; I needed to get my mind off of this stuff. I decided to meet some girlfriends at a local pizza place. I'd met most of these girls through work, although they didn't all still work there.

"So, you're running how far?" one of them asked me.

"Fifty miles," I said.

I watched jaws drop and expressions of confusion emerge. I'd gotten used to this and found it amusing. No one in this group ran much if at all, so this distance far surpassed the rational. I liked that about an ultramarathon over a marathon: most people know someone who has run a marathon, but an ultramarathon? Most non-runners haven't even heard of such a thing.

"You're crazy," another replied.

Half of me enjoyed the reactions; the other half wondered if they were right.

"So, how much are you running now?" one friend asked.

I explained the back-to-back, hoping to hear that this made sense, but I got the same confused expression. I had the wrong audience if I wanted reassurance for any of this.

I said good-bye to my friends and went back home. There was no sense in worrying about this. The back-to-back was just the next challenge in this ultra journey. The weekend would come and I would run it, but not today.

CHAPTER 27

On Friday morning, I headed out to Cottonwood Valley. It was cold—in the thirties! I got out of the car, collected my pack, and started running. The first section was downhill and easily could have gotten away from me. To help keep my pace in check (high nine- and low-ten-minute miles for the first five), I decided to think of this as one thirty-six-miler, rather than back-to-back eighteen-mile runs. This would also help me mentally prepare for the bigger number.

I circled around a mountain on a trail I hadn't taken yet. This was risky—if it turned out to be too technical, I could waste a lot of time traversing it—but it was early in the run and I wanted to explore. There were a lot of quick rollers: up down, up down. It looked great for mountain bikers, not so much for runners. I took a look at the topographical map I had printed out. It looked like this lasted a mile or two, so I continued. I kept my head down to watch for obstacles and ensure I didn't twist an ankle. I heard an unusual noise, like the baying of a sheep. I looked up and spotted a burro on the side of the trail. Then I spotted a few more. The baying continued. I snapped a few pictures and got back to running. I then saw why the baying wouldn't stop: more burros were up the mountain on the other side of the trail. I had to cross between the two mini herds and did so quickly so as not to provoke them.

I ran through the town of Blue Diamond and continued

back into Cottonwood Valley. The sun was fully up now and the mountain face on the west side of the valley was lit up with deep reds and golden yellows. It was beautiful and the crunching of my steps on the trail was peaceful. This part was a gradual uphill, and I kept my pace in the mid elevens. I didn't look at my watch too much to accomplish this; I went off of effort level. I continued to monitor what felt like an easy and sustainable effort and kept me moving forward. I never huffed and puffed, and if I felt my heart starting to pump outside my chest, I slowed down. Because of this, anything steep was a power hike. I needed to practice this technique so that I could use it in the ultra. I used it now to soak up the scenery around me and to take in some fuel and my electrolyte drink mix. I wanted to keep the fueling simple so that I could easily remember it. In a shorter run like this, I could do the math and calculate amounts and make it really complicated, but the ultra could last ten to twelve hours. I wouldn't have the brain power for complicated math. I continued with the plan that had been working: food on the hours, sugar on the half hours. Food consisted of something of value—my sweet potato mix, a Honey Stinger waffle cookie, or a peanut butter and jelly sandwich. Sugar consisted of dried cranberries or gummy candies. I also had prepped a sixteen-ounce Skratch Labs electrolyte mix to replenish my salt content. I drank half of that at about 2.5 hours in and the other half at around 3.5 hours.

At about mile fourteen I saw a huge peace sign made of rocks laid out next to the trail. It perfectly exemplified how I was feeling. Selfie time! After that, it was a gradual uphill back to the start. This was tough and exhausting, but I had enough energy to continue at my easy pace. In the end, I averaged just under eleven minutes per mile. I was happy with that. I felt good—but I had to do this again tomorrow. I didn't feel like I could do that; my aching joints and muscles were ready for a day of rest. Hopefully I would feel different in the morning.

* * *

Excerpt from the Becoming Ultra Podcast
Season 2 Episode 17
How to execute back-to-back long runs
February 5

Scott: Hey, welcome to Becoming Ultra, I'm Scott Jones your host. We are following the journey of Janet from, I'm not gonna say couch to fifty-miler, but we're going from half marathon to a legit fifty-miler. Why don't you guys catch us up on the coaching thing.

Janet: I'm getting to these back-to-back runs. This morning, I did my first half of the back-to-back. I did eighteen this morning. I've got eighteen to do tomorrow. It's incredible because when we started this, I barely was doing eighteen in a week. I can finish these runs and I still have energy, I'm certainly tired and I'm looking forward to a nap, but for the most part, it's everything you guys said it would be. Just take it gradual, watch out for injury, anything that pops up that I notice, I tell Ian about it. It's all about strength training and moving forward.

Scott: Mentally, Janet, what's if feel like to get eighteen done this morning. You seem like a human being right now, not grumpy or weird. You look good, so what's that feel like.

Janet: Believe it or not, this past week, every time I run, I'm in an extremely good mood for the rest of the day. I'm getting past the point where, "Oh my gosh, this sounds like something I can't handle." To, "Okay, yeah, eighteen doesn't seem crazy anymore."

Ian: We've definitely seen big improvements along the way, and that's exactly how it works, it's how the body responds. You have a stimulus, then an adaptation; you have to allow enough recovery and time for that adaptation. So we've had several months already where we've gradually been building up, and now, where earlier the eighteen miles in itself would have been a huge challenge, now you're able to do that, feel pretty normal and be able to do it again the next day. As long as we react to little things that don't feel quite right, whether it's feeling overly tired, or the first hint of something not being quite right, or a minor injury, we want to stop and make sure that we assess what the issue is and whether we need to change your training, rather than just run through it. That's what we've done so far, that's what we did with the initial knee problem.

Scott: So what do you want her to focus on for these big back-to-backs?

Ian: We're trying to simulate running a really long way, so rather than running the thirty-six miles in one go which would be the two eighteen miles combined, it's easier for the body to deal with it in two pieces, but you're still going to be tired on the second day, you don't have a whole lot of recovery. So the second day is more like you are running in the later stage of a really long run. It's a much lower risk of getting injured because you have that recovery and you're not doing it all in one go. You have a higher level of quality in there, because instead of really slowing down and just crawling in at the end of thirty-six miles, instead you're able to keep up a better pace. The pace you start out at in day one, should be the pace you can finish at the end of day one and day two. It's a chance to practice that pacing. It's practicing the food, the drink, the whole strategy that Janet will be using in the fifty-miler. And mentally, it's the confidence to know these things work, that your food and your drink and other tactics are all paying off, that you can pace it, that you can cover this kind of number of miles.

Scott: So, we have people listening right now, they want to go do their first back-to-back weekend. What are a couple of principles to help them put a formula together for their own long runs? Should the back-to-back runs be a distance that's less than their longest run to date?

Ian: Usually a bit less than their longest run. Janet's done a marathon recently, so these back-to-backs at this point are about eighteen. We want to make sure that each of those eighteen miles is mentally digestible.

Janet: The eighteen was definitely a mind thing, where it didn't seem impossible. That was a good distance to pick for me.

Ian: That's just as important as it being physically possible. It's one thing for me to guess what's possible, it's another thing for Janet to accept that it's possible.

Scott: So what are you guys liking about this process so far?

Janet: I like the accountability of it. Doing the social media stuff and having interactions with other people and finding out that there are so many more people that have done ultras than I could possibly ever fathom. It's been eye-opening.

Ian: Seeing that ultras are feasible for anyone, because I have a skewed view on the world where almost everyone I speak to runs ultras. To me, when someone isn't a runner, it's like, oh, that's weird. So, seeing this process, and being able to kind of share that journey to longer runs, and going through all of that again, like I did myself ten years ago, it's really entertaining for me to see the success and the surprise. Because every runner surprises themselves in what they are able to do, the first time they do a marathon, the first time they do an ultra, It's like, "Wow, that is possible." I love coaching people who've not done ultras before.

Scott: I appreciate you guys, as always, just for taking the time for this project. Keep the training up, I'll catch up with you in a couple of weeks, everyone else, you're listening to the Becoming Ultra show. Thanks a lot.

CHAPTER 28

After the podcast, I reflected on the mileages I was running. What used to sound impossibly long now sounded like a day off. Twenty miles? No problem, just needed to do a little planning. It was like a millionaire looking at pocket change: fourteen, seventeen, twenty—was there a difference? I had certainly adapted to this new level of running. I thought about the pacing Ian had mentioned. Because I wasn't running the same route tomorrow, I knew the time of the pacing wouldn't match. I had to concentrate on effort level. Progress forward as strong as possible, without feeling like I was exerting a ton of energy. Walk the steep parts. I told Scott that the accountability was my favorite part of the Becoming Ultra project. I am impressed with people who have trained for an ultra on their own; it really is a long and massive undertaking that needs a long term commitment. I was thankful to be a part of the project to keep me on track.

I woke up the next day and made my normal breakfast: a half portion of oatmeal and a banana with a small cup of coffee. I was hoping to wake up feeling refreshed and energetic, but I felt like I did most days after my long run, stiff and drained. I tended to some blisters between my toes, wrapping them up in numerous Band-Aids. I put my shoes on, looking at the condition of them. They weren't going to make it through the miles I had left in training, much less the miles of the ultra. I would deal with that soon.

I took a last sip of coffee and gathered my pack. I parked at the trailhead and started my eighteen-mile run, just like yesterday. I set out thinking of this as mile nineteen of thirty-six. Within the first mile I ran into my friend Rachel. She was running from a trailhead at the opposite end of the trail, about eight miles away.

She was at her turnaround point, so we ran back toward her car. Spending the next eight miles with Rachel was a welcome relief. It kept my mind off of the massive task I was undertaking, and these miles flew by. When we got to the other end of the trail, she left and I turned around to head back to my car. I was now on mile twenty-eight. All the stiffness I had felt when I woke up was gone. I fell into a rhythm of running and hiking steep sections that felt easy. It was as if my body just gave in and stopped complaining about why this was such a bad idea; it just decided to work for me. At mile thirty-three I reached a section that declined all the way to the end. I felt good and let myself run fast, and I ran the last three miles of this thirty-six-mile run (albeit in two days) incredibly fast: 8:21, 8:44, and 9:41. I couldn't believe it. Ian often said that your body can do more than you think it can, and today was proof of that. I went home with a proud smile on my face, feeling like I'd conquered the world.

CHAPTER 29

Finally, I woke up to a day of rest. I'd earned it, and my body ached appropriately. My hip was still bothering me, and my heels and right Achilles were sore. I'd run a lot of miles in a short time, and normally I would take a couple weeks off before trying something similar. But there was no time, my training schedule showed a twenty-three-miler in less than a week and back-to-back twenty-milers the weekend after that.

I reviewed my training log. Through the marathon, I was running four days a week, and the total mileage reached forty miles. Since recovering from the marathon, I was running five days a week and the total reached into the fifties. My body was understandably worn out. I was tired all the time and needed sleep. Small aches and pains sprouted, and it was tough to determine which were normal and which needed attention. I mentioned them all to Ian.

Feeling as tired as I did, it was difficult to see those upcoming mileages on my schedule and the number of running days and foresee that I would accomplish all of it. However, my first back-to-back showed me that my body can come through for me, even if I don't think it's a good idea. I had to rely on that thinking in the upcoming weeks. I had to refocus and think in small increments—just the next run or two.

There were still two months until the American River

50. I tried to imagine how those miles would feel. The longest I'd run was 26.2—actually, 36 if you counted the back-to-back. However, in the American River 50, there would be no midrace break to sleep for the night. Could I do it? Even once training was done, my longest single run would be just thirty miles. What would miles thirty to fifty really be like? Would my body hold up? I had to trust in the training and the expertise of my coach. This still seemed like an impossible task; I hoped that in the next two months, running fifty miles would start to feel more normal and possible.

The Tuesday after my first back-to-back—like most Tuesdays—I got to the running store early and ran the perimeter of the parking lot, carrying my bright pink canister of pepper spray, armed and ready to fend off the riffraff. Fortunately, I didn't run into any. These miles were easy, and I didn't have any aches or pains.

When I returned to the running store, the group was getting together, and my friend Julie arrived. As we ran, Julie and I chatted. She planned to pace me in the ultra, so we talked about pacing and expectations. She seemed worried about keeping up, and I assured her that wouldn't be a problem. The race website said that pacers weren't allowed on the course until the second half. I told her that if she could walk the distance, that would likely be sufficient at that point. I ran the first mile or so with her, but I was doing a progression run and needed to increase my pace, so at the next mile I said good-bye and then took off, while she kept a slower pace.

The next two and a half miles were uphill, covering a total of three hundred feet of elevation gain. My legs felt strong and I wasn't getting winded; I was able to continue gradually increasing my pace. At the top of the hill, the route turned toward a long downhill. There was about a mile and a half left at this point. Another girl I didn't know was leading the pack, and she was fast. I felt good, still no aches, so I kept up with her. The first half mile went by fast, and when my watch dinged to tell me the mile six split, it read 8:06. Wowsers. One mile left. My form felt right, my cadence was high, and I just let loose. I felt fast and free. The mile sped by, and when my watch dinged for mile seven, it said the most amazing thing—6:49.

I haven't run a mile that fast since I was a kid. My fastest mile ever was 5:35, but I was probably ten years old at the time. Getting sub eight sounded fast, but sub seven? I was forty-three years old; I didn't think that time was possible. When I got home, I walked in with my shoulders back and my chest out. I was proud of my accomplishment. Dan wasn't there—he'd already left for work—so I shared my excitement with my dog instead.

I logged my run into Strava and then went to my closet to put my shoes away. I saw my Hoka One One trail shoes and picked them up. I inspected them and saw lots of wear on the soles. I'd worn these shoes for many miles on rocky trails; they weren't going to make it through all the trail miles left in my training, much less the fifty-mile race. If I wanted to have another shoe choice, I had to get something soon so I could break them in. I put the Hokas down and got ready for work.

After work, I went to REI to look at their shoe selection. I liked my Hokas, but I'd read that in the newest version of my model, they'd narrowed the toe box. That didn't sound comfortable. REI didn't have that shoe, so I couldn't try it and I didn't want to purchase them online without being able to see them. I looked at my other choices and decided on the Brooks Cascadia—a hybrid trail and road shoe, and since the American River 50 had sections of both, I thought this would be a wise choice. The Cascadias had a metal plate built into the sole to protect your feet from terrain—perfect for the trail portions—and they had a good amount of cushioning for the road portions. I'd read that runners changed shoes in the race in between road and trail, but I didn't want to depend on that strategy.

I also wanted to solve my blisters problem. My current strategy was to wrap all my toes in Band-Aids. I heard good things about the Injinji toesocks. They look like gloves for your feet. I was hoping to combat my problem without having to personally be responsible for Band-Aid's quarterly profits, so I picked up a pair of the toesocks. I also purchased more Honey Stinger waffle cookies and gummies.

I planned to try the new gear on my next run, which was just one twenty-three-miler; it was weird that sounded easy now. I knew I should only try one new variable on a run, but I was running out of time—the race was in less than two months.

CHAPTER 30

The day before my twenty-three-miler, there were cupcakes at work. I knew with my long run the next day I shouldn't eat them, but I couldn't help myself; I had more than my share. With all the training I'd already done, I thought this run would be easy, and I wanted them. A lot of them.

On my long run day, I had my normal breakfast, put on my new toesocks and trail shoes, and set out. I wanted to revisit the stretch of trail I'd been avoiding since the beginning of my training—the Amargosa trail. It was about a two-and-a-half-mile stretch, which would make five miles total out and back. When I finished that, I could change out my shoes.

I met with Rachel and we ran toward the tough trail section. It was early. The sun hadn't risen over the mountains yet, and the air was cool. The trail was difficult like I remembered, and we power-hiked the steep parts. I didn't have much energy and just felt drained. It might have been the difficulty of the trail, but I suspected the cupcakes were to blame and began to regret my splurge.

Rachel told me about a book she was reading about a genie in the desert. I looked around and did not find one in reality, but I liked the story. The first five miles passed quickly, and the shoes felt good. I considered changing them out but decided to keep them on and get a jump on breaking them in. After a few more miles, I started to feel the rocks through the soles more than normal. I reminded myself that these were not meant solely for trails, and the trail at American River 50 wouldn't be so rocky. Rachel turned around and I was on my own.

Shortly thereafter, the rocks under my feet became painful. I was eight miles from my car, so I had to continue. As my feet revolted against each step, my knees joined in on the complaints. The pain got more and more prominent with each slow mile. With at least an hour left to go, I ran out of nutrition so I couldn't get an energy boost.

I got to the top of the final saddle of the trail and started a three-mile gradual descent to the trailhead. I should have been able to cruise through this, but the constant pain prevented that. Even though my legs were stronger than ever and my muscles were taking much more of the effort than they used to, the pain in my feet and knees overshadowed my every thought. Each mile got slower and I just wanted the run to end.

I finally got back to my car and took the shoes off. These were not going to be my race shoes. Maybe if I'd eased into them they would have worked, but it was too late for that now. I was never putting these shoes back on. I had back-to-back twenty-milers the next weekend and my thirty-miler the following weekend. I was stuck. I didn't have a pair of shoes I thought could take the upcoming miles and the ultra. I took the toesocks off and inspected my toes. No blisters! Well, that was a pleasant surprise. At least there was something salvageable from this run.

The next day, I had a two-hour hike scheduled. I put on my marathon finisher's jacket. I grabbed my dog and headed to the Amargosa trail, the beast of a trail I had run the day before. I set out on an uphill climb and let my dog follow at her own pace. She stopped once in a while to sniff out something of interest. I walked ahead and whistled to her from time to time to have her catch up.

I thought about my run the previous day. I finished it, and that was important, but I sabotaged myself on many points. I ate poorly the day before and chose to wear those shoes for too long. I had to take my runs seriously and be more conscious of the choices I was making. In particular, I needed to eat better the day before my challenging runs. I didn't want to be super strict about my diet—I wasn't going to eat all greens the day before and avoid all junk food—but I didn't need to make such bad choices like overloading on sugary cupcakes. I decided that I would at least limit junk food the day before long runs and maintain a healthy balance the rest of the time. I wanted running to be a fun part of my life, not the thing that controlled me.

Plus, I was four months into this training, and I was tired. I was starting to feel like I had done enough already. Physically, I was so much stronger than I'd been at the start, but I was also feeling run down. I needed my sleep more than ever. I was also worn out mentally; I just wanted to get off the training grind.

I turned around to check on my dog and didn't see her right away. I whistled and saw her head perk up over a rock. I whistled again and she came running toward me.

Ian said that I would see some huge improvements in my fitness in the next two months. Being as physically fit as possible could only help me in the ultra. Ian mentioned that many things can go wrong in an ultra I surmised he meant my legs could cramp, my gut could revolt, or I could trip and twist an ankle. I planned to stick to his training plan to give myself the biggest advantage possible.

My twenty-three-miler was only three miles short of the marathon distance I had run the month before. After the marathon, I was praised for such a huge accomplishment, and I was allowed four days' rest before doing a test run to see how my legs felt. Now I was supposed to do six miles just two days after my twenty-three-miler. What happened to celebrating a huge feat? This was just business as usual now, which was disappointing to say the least. I reminded myself this was ultra training, not post-marathon achievement hour.

As I made the final descent of the trail, my dog trotted along behind me. We got to the trailhead and I looked back at the mountain trail we'd just climbed. I smiled and gave my dog a good scratch on her back.

CHAPTER 31

Beep. Beep. Beep. My alarm went off and I opened my eyes. Pitch black surrounded me. I shut off the alarm and then checked my phone for the outside temperature—mid-forties. It was Tuesday and I had to get up for a run. I stretched my feet, fanning my toes back and forth, then pointing them, and then flexing my foot back. After long runs, my heels were tight in the morning and the first few steps were painful. Even though it was a few days later, they were still sore. I found this routine eased the stiffness and made getting out of bed easier.

After my stretching routine, I got up and went to the balcony to see what it was like outside. I opened the slider and a cold blast hit me. *I'm going to freeze my butt off out there.* Then I remembered that Krystal was training for this same ultra in Buffalo, where temps were below freezing. I thought about training in that weather, the number of layers I'd need, the way my toes would feel, the burn of the cold in my lungs. *OK, I don't have it too bad.* I needed to remember Krystal running in the cold anytime I wanted to complain about the temperature.

I went to my closet, put my running clothes on, grabbed the pepper spray and some cold weather gear, and then went to the kitchen to fill a water bottle. All steps that were part of a well-oiled machine at this point. I drove to the running group's meet-up spot; put on my ear wrap, hat, and gloves; and got out of the car to run my extra miles around the parking lot's perimeter. As I ran, I looked around and found this to be incredibly boring. It was dark and cold and I was alone and didn't want to be here. Would I be doing this if it wasn't for the ultra? Would I be doing this if a coach wasn't telling me I had to? No, of course not. I wanted to run in beautiful scenery and enjoy myself. This was not fun.

I tried to remember my resolve from yesterday, that I had to continue to take my training seriously. I wasn't done yet, I wasn't ready to run the ultra yet, but this was just so mundane and cold. As I ran, my nose dripped and I took out a tissue to take care of it.

However, I wasn't going to be able to do the fun, scenic runs over treacherous terrain if I didn't put in the work. When I think of running, I think of all the high points, but that morning was the boring part—the real training, the part that would make me strong and capable and allow me to run impressive races without getting injured.

After a mile, I ran back to the meet-up point where runners were gathering. I told myself to get my head straight and joined the group for the rest of my run.

Despite the pep talk to myself, a seed of doubt invaded my mind. *Do I really want to be doing all this? I could just stop.* I kept this thought at a superficial level. I couldn't stop thoughts like this from surfacing, they had been occurring to me for some time now, but I could keep them from gaining a foothold. I fought off this thought by thinking about why I started all of this to begin with. I wanted to have an adventure. To accomplish something that seemed impossible, but that I could be proud that I'd done it. But this kind of a challenge, to run fifty miles, takes time. I had to see this through.

I needed to get my mind off of the larger philosophical questions of this project, so I concentrated on some of the details. The week before the twenty-miler back-to-backs, I evaluated my gear. I decided to order a pair of the newer model of Hoka One One Stinson. Even if they were a bit narrow in the toe, I liked their cushioning, and after my experiment with the

Brooks Cascadia, I didn't have time to try out another brand. I got on the internet and placed the order. Hopefully they would arrive before this weekend and I could try them. With that settled, my shoe dilemma was hopefully over.

I was happy with my hydration pack; however, the mouthpiece of the bladder had developed a small leak. I looked online for a replacement part and couldn't find it. So I went to REI, they did not have just the mouthpiece, so I had to get a whole replacement bladder. Once I got back home and tried to put it in my pack, I realized that it didn't fit. Back to square one. Maybe it wouldn't get worse. I'd feel better if I had a backup, but replacement bladders weren't cheap, nor was buying a whole new pack. I tabled this problem.

I assessed my nutrition plan. My plan remained simple: food on the hours and sugar on the half hours. For the food, I was happy with my sweet potato mix. I tried it once with a little peanut butter added in for a little extra protein, but I didn't like it, so I stuck with my original recipe. I made small pancakes once, but they were dry and became a choking hazard when I tried to eat while running. I tried chocolate chip cookies and those worked great. Maybe I was biased because I just love cookies, but they really did work. For the sugars, I liked dried cranberries and gummy candies. I tried Coke and that worked well. I heard that it would be available on the American River 50 course. I also tried chia seeds in an energy drink, along with water, lemon, and honey. I liked that combination, but it didn't seem practical to use.

I had noticed that while I was running, when I started to feel fatigued, like my muscles were getting heavy, if I took in some nutrition, almost immediately I felt better and had energy. I had to remember that correlation when I was in the ultra: I didn't have to get bogged down by feeling tired because there was something I could do about it.

So I had my gear mostly in line. My nutrition plan was working; I just had to make sure to bring enough. If I had all of this working for my long runs now, it should work for the ultra as well. I started preparing myself mentally for the back-to-back the upcoming weekend.

CHAPTER 32

For my first twenty-miler of the weekend, I chose Cottonwood Valley and pulled into my parking spot—by this time in the training, I felt like I could call a spot mine. That, and no one else was there at 6:45 a.m. on a Friday. I stepped out of the car and the cold morning air bit me. It was February and it was in the low forties, but once I got going it would be comfortable, so I didn't adjust my clothing choices. I got my pack on and set out. My new shoes hadn't arrived yet, so I wore my old Hokas.

I sped along faster than I should, but I felt light and free so I let go. The sun was already up casting long shadows of the cacti and rocks across the trail. Sections near the base of crags were shaded and chilly. I pressed on.

A steep section past halfway allowed me to power-hike and conserve some energy. The massive sandstone cliffs towered over me. I welcomed the walk so I could look up at them. This trail gave me a sense of peace and calm. I took out my sweet potato mix and ate it. My muscles felt refreshed from the starches. The miles passed by and eventually I headed back down the valley toward my car.

When I finished, I took my shoes off and peeled away my Injinji toesocks. Again, no blisters, these would definetly be my race socks. None of my pain areas panged, no crises occurred, and I felt reasonably good.

I got in my car and checked my phone. Some friends from the Run Grrrls Run group wanted to get together that night. They planned to go indoor rock climbing. My heart sank. I wanted to hang out, but rock climbing? I wondered if that was a good idea with another twenty-miler in the morning. If I weren't training, I would have been so excited.

I got home and unpacked everything and then slept on the couch for a few hours. After getting up, I decided to meet up with Corrina, Jenny, and Julie. While I was there, I tried to take it easy and not climb too much. It looked like such fun, climbing all over the place, finding hand holds and taking chances. I kept thinking about the run the next day so I held back from climbing and concentrated on the camaraderie.

* * *

Excerpt from the Becoming Ultra Podcast
Season 2 Episode 19
Mid training shoe changes, a sub 7 mile, and takeaways after 100 miles
February 19

Scott: Hey, welcome to Becoming Ultra. So, Janet, last time we were together, we talked about your really long back-to-back eighteen-milers. Since then, what has your training looked like?

Janet: I had a lot of anxiety about going out the second day because I didn't feel fresh, this is going to be tough. But the running really fell into a rhythm way easier, much quicker and sooner in the run. My mile splits were so much better than they'd been the day before. I felt really, really good. So, today, I did twenty this morning, and I'll do twenty tomorrow, so I'm nowhere near as concerned about it as I was last time.

Ian: Compare that to the last time you did a twenty mile run.

Janet: Completely different, I don't want to say easier, because twenty miles is never easy, this just all felt a lot more fitting than it had in the past.

Ian: I think that's showing your increase in fitness overall.

Scott: So what are the plans for Janet moving forward here. Her health seems to be pretty good, I think there's forty some days before the race right now. So Ian, are you just gonna keep increasing the volume, what's the goal?

Ian: We're not just increasing volume for the sake of it. She's got a lot this week because of the fact that she's got the two back-to-back twenty-milers. We're not just going to keep going up from there, it's more that we're gonna enter in more quality in those long runs. So just regularly getting long runs that are now twenty miles is not a big deal, while when we first did that is was. Next weekend is a thirty mile run. You just want to have, not just the physical capability, which we're getting from these long runs and the time on her feet that she's getting, but also the mental side of it. For a fifty-miler, I think it helps to have done something longer than the marathon, even if only marginally, because it just makes everything seem that much more feasible. There's no benefit in doing a forty-five mile run in the buildup because then you've basically done the race, but it is does help to do something a little bit more than the marathon. It's more for the confidence building knowing that there's nothing scary beyond that marathon distance and it still works exactly the same way.

Scott: You guys were talking about shoes when we were off air, so what were you guys talking about specifically.

Janet: I'm trying to figure out what shoes I want to wear for the race. I normally wear Hoka One One's for trails and Brooks for street. But my Hokas are getting worn out so I wanted to get a new pair of trail shoes and break them in. I thought maybe because the American River 50 didn't seem as technical as what I'm used to maybe the Brooks trail shoes would be fine. So I bought those, ran my twenty-three-miler in them, the entire thing in them last week. I did figure out that those shoes are not going to work, they do not have the kind of cushioning that I'm used to. When I'm running over rocks, I want something more. So I went back to the Hokas today, and the run was fine. So I'm definitely gonna stick with the Hokas, but then my concern is if these are kind of worn out, am I supposed to wear these? I ordered new Hokas, is there time at this point to break them in?

Ian: In general, it's good to break shoes in. But these days they're more flexible than they used to be, so it's not like a pair of dress shoes that you really do have to break in. You can often go straight out of the box. I wouldn't recommend doing a race with shoes that you've never worn before. It makes sense for Janet to have a pair that has been worn in for at least one long run, just to make sure that they feel fine. It makes sense to do that now while we've got about six weeks to build up to it gradually and make sure that everything with her gear, shoes, hydration, everything is tried and tested and we can trust it and we know it's gonna work.

Scott: For me, when I'm picking a shoe, if I feel like I have to break it in, then I usually don't go with it.

Ian: And it's not about just breaking it in, it's about making sure they are comfortable. And that's not quite the same thing. It's checking that they work as we expect them to, because there's no benefit in turning up on race day and not having things that you could have tested but chose not to. In particular, the most important thing for a pair of shoes, is that they're comfortable. Otherwise, that's a long time to be in something that's annoying you, or causing blisters, or just doesn't feel right.

Scott: So Ian, you ran the Rocky Raccoon 100 miler a couple of weeks ago, you have some takeaways.

Ian: Rocky Raccoon loops, so you have five twenty mile loops, and some out and back sections. So normally, in a point to point, you don't see anyone. At Rocky Raccoon, you get to see the guy in last place, the guy who's struggling, the guy who's doing really well and going through good and bad patches. You see each and every runner multiple times. Because of that, you get to see how the entire field is approaching a race. These are things that are going to be very applicable for American River, is that people always start out too quickly. In a five loop race, if your last loop takes twice as long as your first loop, you know you've screwed it up a little bit. If you ran your first loop, and your fifth loop is a death march, you've made some error in how you've approached the race. The people who looked best when I saw them later on in the race, where the ones who'd strategically been choosing to do power hiking, who had been chatting to people, and just being very relaxed in the early stages.

Janet: In the very beginning of the race, it's going to be extremely tough to go slower, because you feel good. So how do you know if when you're going slow enough?

Ian: Good question. Ultimately, for something like this fifty-miler, I would suggest, as long as you feel comfortable, that's slow enough. If you go super slow and you're really holding yourself back, it's not necessarily going to be more efficient, it'll just take you longer. As long as you're relaxed and you don't feel like you're pushing at all, and a good way of judging it is if you're actually able to have the occasional conversation. If you can do that, then you're probably in a relaxed enough pace that it is more sustainable.

Scott: So Janet, do not go out and run your sub-seven minute mile. So tell us about that, is this the first time you have ever run that fast before?
Janet: As an adult, yes. I didn't really think that was possible at this age. It was a run after my back-to-back eighteen-milers. It was downhill, but it just felt great to open up my stride, to run free and fast. Everything just came together. The mile split was a 6:49.

Scott: You can't get there without putting the time in. It's still an aerobic event. So, your fitness is definitely getting better. And your nervous system, intermuscular, they're catching up, too. You can take tons of runners and put them on a downhill, but they still have to have the nervous system to turn those legs over. Those are good signs.

Ian: Exactly, we're seeing the fitness come through. We're seeing improvements in the endurance, in the speed. Everything is paying off.

Scott: As always, thanks a lot, thanks for your time. I appreciate you listening.

CHAPTER 33

The next morning I went to the McCullough Hills Trail. I started with a five-mile out and back on Amargosa. By this point in the training, I no longer avoided this tough section. Upon returning, I set out for the remaining fifteen miles as another out and back on the main trail. I knew this trail like the back of my hand. I knew where the steep patches were, I knew the layout of the surrounding mountains, and I knew the easier parts where the trail descended. I knew where in the trail I could see the Las Vegas Strip in the distance. So much activity was constantly going on down there, but up here I had the mountains all to myself. I loved being out here, and it felt like home.

My knee hurt for a while, and then the pain went away. My Achilles hurt for a while, and then that pain went away, too. This run was harder than the day before, but I surprised myself and completed it without any massive setbacks. I'd just done forty miles in two days, and I could still walk. I felt good, all things considered. *Maybe I really can do fifty in one day?* It felt like maybe it was feasible.

I drove home, and when I got out of the car, I felt a sharp pain in my right heel. *Oh no, now what?* I took a few steps, and it hurt with each one. I hobbled up to my apartment, set my foot in an ice bath, and sent an email to Ian.

My heel pain subsided by the next day for the most part, I

had already been dealing with heel pain in the morning after my long runs, but it now became a daily problem when first getting out of bed. Ian did not sound the alarms; he said to monitor it and let him know if anything changed.

I had bigger problems. That week I had a work-related in-town conference for which I had obligations every day. From the start of training, I knew this was going to be my one big scheduling conflict. I took out the conference schedule and my training schedule. The conference ran all day Monday through Thursday and half day on Friday, and I had to drive to the strip every day, which added more time. That week's training included a five-miler, two seven-mile trail runs, a four-miler, and my thirty-miler on Saturday. I took a deep breath and started planning.

I could get up early on Monday and do the five-miler and even earlier on Tuesday for the seven-mile trail run. Late afternoon on Wednesday I could fit in another seven miles on trail; it would be hot out, but I needed some heat training, right? Thursday just wouldn't work; there was no free time. So that left Friday for the four-miler. Then, after all that, I would run the trail marathon on Saturday with a four-mile warm-up. *Who does that? Seriously, have I lost my mind?* I pushed the conference schedule and my computer away from me. It was going to be a very busy week.

So far, I'd been able to fit in all Ian had set out for me. I was paying good money to have a coach work out all the details, so it was my job to fit it all in. I could have skipped a run in this busy week; Ian said that it would be fine if I missed some runs, but I knew any effort I put in now would make me more prepared for the ultra. I wanted the race to hurt as little as possible. That meant doing the work now. If I started skipping runs, even for a good reason like this conference, what other reasons would I come up with to skip runs? *No*, I told myself. *The schedule is worked out. Don't think about it again.* I would take each day as it came, run the runs, and attend the conference.

My new Hokas arrived on Tuesday during the conference,

but I already had enough stress that I didn't wear them for any of the runs. I tried them on, and they felt comfortable, although the toe box was narrow just like I had heard. The conference week ended and it all worked out—I fit in all my runs and conference obligations. After Friday's run, I went to Desert Dash's packet pickup for the Blood, Sweat and Beers race. After this weekend, I only had one back-to-back left and then it was time to taper for the fifty-miler. It was only five weeks away.

I got home from packet pickup, took my bib out of the race packet, and laid out my Flat Janet on the couch: my favorite maroon shorts were topped with a turquoise stripped shirt, my Buff headband sat above my shirt, and my Injinji toesocks below my shorts with my old Hokas. No way was I going to wear the new ones for my thirty-miler. Soon I would be doing this for my first ultra. I wondered what would happen after all this, after I didn't feel obligated to a schedule. What kind of runner would I be? I felt like a super woman right now. I could pick a distance and run it. I liked that a lot. I do better with a goal than with running just for the fun of it, but maybe after this I should do some just-for-the-fun-of-it time to see what I like about that. I looked at my completed Flat Janet and felt satisfied that I was ready. Or as ready as I could be for someone going to run thirty miles for the first time ever.

CHAPTER 34

I arrived early to the Blood, Sweat, and Beers race and got a prime parking spot right by the finish line. No other runners were there yet; it wasn't likely anyone else was doing a three-mile warm up for a twenty-seven-mile race. (Yes, the marathon was posted as longer than a marathon. Fine by me, less I had to do on my own.)

I ran three miles down a paved bike path at the slowest pace I could make myself go, and then returned to the car to wait for the real race to start.

I opened up my trunk and removed my pack. I took out a 33Shake chia seed mix, added some water to it, and ate it. I wanted to run at a twelve-minute pace for the race. My three-mile warm-up was closer to eleven minutes. Choosing a pace or race time had nothing to do with competing for me. I truly just wanted to finish the race with as little pain as possible. However, it was helpful for me to set a goal so that I knew how to start the race. Beth, who I'd run with out at Cowboy Trails, said to go out slow. That seemed to be the overwhelming advice I'd received for all my long runs. This was a difficult thing. I was so trained up that going slow took effort. I felt so good in the beginning; it was easy to convince myself to run fast first while I could, since there would be some slow miles at the end. I decided to heed the advice of those who'd done this before and force myself to go slow. Beth also said that if I could run this trail marathon, I'd be fine for the fifty-miler. If I didn't die here, at least I'd gain a little confidence going into the ultra.

I got the last of my supplies and donned my pack. I shut the trunk and headed for the start line. I looked around at the other people lined up. These were the hard-core runners. Everyone wore trail shoes, Buff-style headbands, and hydration packs. At other trail races I'd looked at the marathon runners with respect and envy. Now I was one of them. Pride sent a wave of warmth through my body—or was that the sun that was just beginning to peek over the mountains?

The gun went off and I set out on the course. At most trail races I jockeyed for position trying to get ahead of runners I thought I'd be faster than, but not today. I forced myself to settle in and go slow. The first few miles went great, except for veering off the course at one point and having to double back to get back on. I circled around a lower section of the course and had an expansive view of Lake Mead. The early morning light cast a sense of hopefulness and possibilities.

Just after mile nine, I started a two-mile stretch with close to eight hundred feet in elevation gain. I ran what I could, but once I hit a set of switchbacks at the top, I power-hiked what I had to. I was feeling good, no stress points. I snapped a few pictures and kept going.

The next ten or so miles passed and my confidence grew. I felt good and was navigating the terrain well. My nutrition was holding up and I ate some candy and potato chips at the aid stations. By midday, it was hot but I didn't mind it. My water supply and electrolyte drink mix were working well.

I hit an aid station with about seven miles to go. They had peanut butter and jelly sandwiches and I snarfed one down. It tasted like the best thing I'd ever eaten in my whole life. I needed the energy because the last loop included the two-mile stretch with the eight-hundred-foot climb and the switchbacks again. I ran as far as I could up the steep part, but my walks were more frequent and longer than they'd been the first time around. I looked around; since I was walking, I didn't have to watch my footing so carefully. The first time through the sun had lit up this whole area; now there were shadows from the other direction. I spotted a few longhorn sheep scaling a rocky area. I watched them unbelievably place hooves into nooks and crannies of what looked like a rockslide to me. At one point, one of them slid down about ten feet but recovered and continued with the herd.

After struggling up the switchbacks, I was at about twenty-six miles; only four miles remained. Once again, I was about to complete the longest run of my life. The sun was waning in the sky and it started to feel like the day was slipping away. I looked at my watch; I was six hours in. I'll admit it—I was bored. I felt like I had spent enough time doing a single activity for one day. How long would the fifty-miler take me? Ten hours? Eleven? Twelve? That was twice as long! But I wasn't done yet, so I cleared my mind and got back to work. The last loop was tough and I was tired. My ability to keep steady on my feet was dwindling. There was a stretch of tough bike rollers near the end, a constant up down, up down. Both of my knees hurt, but I didn't want to stop. Starting back up again seemed even more impossible, so I just kept going. One foot in front of the other.

Then I got to the finish line and was handed a beer—it was Blood, Sweat, and Beers after all. I stood in the finish area looking back at the mountains I'd spent all day traversing. The sun was heading into the western sky and I felt good, in an accomplished sense, despite my body hurting and being completely drained of energy. I took a sip of beer and smiled. Thirty miles. When this ultra project started, Ian told me that my longest training run would be thirty miles, and now it was done. As I took a long sip of beer, I thought about the one looming problem: my knees hurt, my heels hurt, and the thought of walking to the car sounded awful. It wasn't possible that I could go twenty more miles, was it?

* * *

Excerpt from the Becoming Ultra Podcast
Season 2 Episode 21

A first timers approach to being paced during a fifty-miler
March 3

Scott: Alright everybody, welcome to Becoming Ultra. I'm Scott Jones your host. Ian, why don't you coach her up a little bit, let us know what's been going on the last couple of weeks, and what's coming up in the next couple of weeks as well.

Ian: Janet has, each week, gone into new territory. We had a thirty-miler, so longest run of Janet's life. It now makes the marathon she did seem like it's old hat. So, how did the extra long run go?

Janet: It went really well. I went out really intending to go slow, control the pacing, control the effort. It felt really slow in the beginning. I was probably doing eleven to eleven-thirty pace, so that I would have energy left at the end. It was really hard to judge how much effort to put forth and still conserve and have something left at the end. By the end, I was going pretty slow, I was going twelve, thirteen, maybe even thirteen-thirty pace. So it wasn't nearly as fast as I had anticipated it would be or wanted it to be, but I felt great. I had energy left at the end. I still had strength left in my legs to take the downhills. I was very happy with it.

Ian: I think it's exactly what we needed here. We were trying to get into the mindset of, try and do thirty miles, but with the aim that you could do more than that. So the fact that your legs were feeling good, and you were able to pace it well, there wasn't too much slowing down. And bear in mind that we've also got more time to see improvements, to get physical developments from that run itself. So that's exactly what we needed.

Scott: A lot of runners will draw their confidence from their pace. Janet, just hearing you talking about having confidence from not having your legs get really worn out on the downhill, for an ultra runner, that is a much bigger confidence builder.

Ian: In an ultra, you've gotta make sure you're picking a speed and an effort level that is sustainable. It's all about efficiency and sustainability. It's all about being able to run well in the later stages of the race, and the way you do that is by constantly asking yourself, "Does this feel right? Do I need to take it a little bit easier? Do I need to eat a bit more? Do I need to look after myself in the heat?" There's a million questions you've got to be constantly asking and checking up on yourself. And if something does go a little bit wrong, you adjust it before it goes to the point where it is very difficult to fix. So, in terms of the pacing for the race, the second half of the race, you're gonna have other people to help pace you, so what are your plans for that? Who's going to be helping you out?

Janet: I don't think there's a definite plan, yet. My brother plans to do about fifteen miles of the second half. No one can pace in the first half. And a friend is planning on coming out so hopefully she'll take up about ten miles of that, too. So I don't really have a plan with that, I've told them, I think they think I'll be going faster than I am. It's kind of hard to judge. I know my brother runs at a really fast pace, so for him to dial it down might be difficult. I guess we'll have to wait and see.

Ian: That's one thing the pacers usually think, especially if someone's been training more than they have. They think there's no way they'll keep up with you. It's not exactly lightning quick in the later stages of an ultra. It's still important that the pacers are runners, and whatever distance they are doing, they are going to be really comfortable with that. The last thing you want to be doing is worrying about how they are feeling, when you're already going through a whole load of things. It's all about them looking after you, and you don't want to have any worries about them. Let them know what you expect of them. Do you want them to be in front of you, do you want them to be behind, do you want them to talk to you, do you want them to be silent, do you want them to be constantly giving you motivational things about how great you are and how awesome it's going, or do you want them to just say nothing ever. The problem is if you don't make those things clear and they feel the need to do certain things that just annoy you.

Janet: These are all things that I hadn't thought about.

Scott: I think the first question people are asking is the decision to have a pacer or not. That decision comes from where you draw your energy. Do you feel energized with people around you, or do you really prefer when you're out there by yourself?

Ian: It's more mental energy than physical. You still gotta power your legs. Do you think it would be helpful to have someone there for moral support, or to be able to speak to the volunteers at aid stations? It helps to have someone to help you stick to your plan, in that way, and just make things a little bit more relaxed and take some of the hassles out of it, but again, it's very much a personal preference of, do you think these things would help, or would you rather just be on your own.

Janet: You bring up a lot of things that I've got to be honest, I never even thought about. It's hard to know if I'll do better with it or without it. I'm looking at it more like, after half of this is over, I'll take any help I can get.

Scott: So, we're gonna switch gears a little bit, Ian, what did you do to yourself?

Ian: I was doing a run, and I twisted my ankle. It's one week before I have a marathon, so I'm now trying to decide whether or not to go to it. Because although I can run, does it feel good enough to run twenty-six hard miles? This is not a big focus race for me, so it's that call that every runner needs to make. If things aren't quite perfect, do you risk making yourself get more injured? Hopefully we won't have this issue in the final month with Janet, but there could be the same kind of thing where something feels just a little bit off, do you still do the long run? It's all about keeping your eye on the prize, what are the main things you want to do with running in the next few months, so would continuing to run on it harm it or help it?

Scott: Are you swollen?

Ian: It's not swollen, no, I can run on it fine. It just doesn't feel quite perfect. I think I'd be safe to run it, but it's that fine line. I mean, if it's swollen, then there's a clear answer.

Scott: So what does Janet's next few weeks look like?

Ian: Basically, the aim from here, we're about a month out, so we have a couple of more weeks of increasing the workload just a little bit. Then the final two weeks will be tapering.

Scott: Janet, are you excited for this?

Janet: Yeah. It's just an impressive thing to see. When I first talked to Ian, I'm like, "Are you sure this is something that I can do?" Now that I'm this far along in this, I only have a couple of more weeks, and then I'm trained. I can see it, I can see actually being able to do it now.

Ian: It's amazing what the human body can do, and you're seeing it firsthand. A lot of people don't push their body enough to realize how much it can adapt and improve. It's not an easy process, but it's something anyone can do.

Scott: Really good clients, that follow the program to a tee, they are always surprised at how well it works. The ones that don't follow through, they're not surprised that it isn't working. They're just assuming it wasn't going to work in the first place.

Ian: It's really been paying off. The hard work has got us almost to race day, you've got a little bit more. I'm sure when we talk in a couple of weeks, you'll be itching to get this race out of the way.

Scott: You guys, thanks so much for listening. Hope you guys learned something today.

CHAPTER 35

Since deciding to run fifty miles, I had read and heard a lot of advice, and when I couldn't figure something out, I kept falling back on one piece in particular: "Trust the process." The primary reason I appreciated having a coach for this race is that I didn't have to come up with what I needed to do. Ian set out a few weeks in advance for me, and then created more depending on how I was doing. I trusted that he had seen others go from a half marathon to fifty miles, and if he said what I was doing would get me there, I believed him. At the end of the thirty-miler, I didn't see how I could have run another mile. But I had to put the *how* out of my head and continue to trust the process—and Ian. I found a lot of ultra training is mind-control training. I didn't learn to move things remotely, although that would be really cool, but I did learn to train my mind not to dwell on things that are way too big for me to figure out. I knew that would be a helpful skill for many things in life, not just running.

Another piece of advice that made sense to me is "The more the merrier." If one person would be good for a project, more can only make it better. When this project started, lots of people showed interest in being a part of it with me. They wanted to pace and crew: they would either run with me for parts of the ultra or be at aid stations with supplies. I thought, sure, how could that not be helpful? Because it was in Sacramento and I lived in Vegas, however, I doubted many—if any—would actually be able to go. Still, I welcomed the interest. My mom had taken me to all my races as a kid, but she couldn't be at my marathon; she swore she was going to be at my fifty-miler. It was humbling to have people want to be there, and I told anyone interested, no problem, come on down.

During the last podcast, Scott and Ian discussed crew and pacers. They brought up some issues that had not occurred to me. Pacers can't be a hindrance to me; they have to be aware of the course and be prepared to run the entire section they choose to do. I thought about Julie. She had been planning to pace me but had gotten injured recently. What if she said she could do it, but once she got out there, she couldn't? What if I had to stop to take care of her? My brother Tom said he was coming and wanted to pace me, too. There were only three legs to divvy up; who should get which leg? Scott and Ian mentioned that my crew should be able to foresee what I might need and know where to drive to aid stations. I thought about my mom, who was in pretty good shape but not as spry as she once was. I couldn't be giving her directions while I was running. Dan was also planning to go, and he would spend more time with my mom than I would.

That podcast discussion filled me with anxiety. Every race I'd run in the last twenty years, I was solo. At the marathon, Krystal and Alison were there, but we were all running our own races and were not responsible for each other. I had no one to worry about except myself. The race distances were never far enough to worry about carrying water, much less needing a pair of shoes to change into. Did I want pacers? Did I want crew? Would these just cause more stress to an already stressful day?

I tried to push these concerns from my mind using my new mind-control techniques, but this wasn't like the other aspects of this training. These were people who cared about me and were willing to take time out of their lives to help me with this feat. I didn't want to hurt anyone's feelings, so I decided to let everybody do what they wanted to do.

The weekend after the thirty-miler I headed out for a sixteen-miler. I was trying out the new Hokas, hopefully this final part of my gear would work. I took a deep breath and tried to piece together how this would all work. I needed to rent a car with enough space for crew and pacers. I needed to figure out how to get my fresh foods to Sacramento. Should I cook it ahead of time or once I was there? Would sweet potato mash make it through security? Or should I check the bag it was in? I needed to find out airport arrival times and who would pick up whom. I needed to plan out the race course, where crew could be, what I needed when. This was all like vacation planning on steroids! My thoughts about the ultra itself—the open air, the all-day endurance challenge, the thrill of crossing the finish line—were all clouded in these details. I finished my run in some pain—nothing severe, but more than usual. Maybe it was the new Hokas, however they felt comfortable on my feet. *Who knows at this point.* My joints ached all over, and my muscles burned in a way I'd never felt before. The stress of planning everything was adding to my fatigue; I just wanted some rest, but there was no relief yet. I was spent, and I had the last step in the training next weekend: a back-to-back twenty-two-miler.

CHAPTER 36

When the weekend came I was still fatigued. I usually did my first back-to-back run on Friday, but when I mentioned to Ian how drained I felt, he said to wait an extra day. *Really? Is one day going to make a difference?* If I wasn't going to run, I had to find something to do. I looked around my apartment. Dan had been picking up my slack and the place was immaculate. I decided to do an extra clean job on the kitchen. I moved everything from the counters and got into the corners. I cleaned the cabinets and the fridge. I got everything back into place. I let out a big sigh. That took twenty minutes. Now what? Since I was expecting to run twenty-two miles today, I had so much extra time. Lately, all I wanted was more time to rest, now that I had it, I couldn't sit still.

I made plans to meet up with some girlfriends for lunch. We discussed what we'd been up to. They asked me questions about the ultra. I didn't have anything new to say. As with the marathon, I was to the point where I was ready to get to it. They turned the discussion to calories and losing weight. I'd ordered double what they had with no concern for healthy choices, as my appetite was huge these days. I sat there with a half grin and stayed out of the discussion. It felt good to not have to worry about calories.

When I got home, I sat down to plan where I would run the next day. I was growing tired of the same routes and wanted something to peak my interest. I was fortunate to live where there were choices for these long runs. I took out a map of the Red Rock Canyon area. It was the scenic park on the west end of the valley where I'd run my trail half marathon in one hundred degrees temps not too long ago. I was so much more prepared now. I mapped out a huge loop that would give me my first twenty-two-miler.

When I woke up the next day, I felt so much better. The extra day had done the trick. Maybe it was the extra healing time, but I think it was the ability to give myself a break from the schedule. Even if it was only one day, it felt relieving to know that this training had some wiggle room. I set out for Red Rock Canyon. The main parking lot wasn't open when I arrived shortly after 6 a.m. I'd gotten information about a small parking lot just outside the park and started there. The start of this route was on a trail that I'd never been on. The first section was rocky and the trail wasn't obvious at times. I was glad it was at the beginning, before my body was tired so that I could have fun with it.

After about ten miles, I ran through a popular part of the park where people were climbing all over the red rock formations. I smiled and wondered what they would say if they knew how far I'd run today and how far I planned to run a few weeks from now. At about mile sixteen, I circled back and ran up the part that had been the final stretch of my half marathon. It was hot, but not as hot as it'd been on that day. I had so much more energy. I wondered how I would do if I ran that race today.

At about mile nineteen, I made the final turn that put me in the direction of the car, and then a truth started to nag me: the car was farther than I predicted. I tried to block out the thought, but as each mile ticked by, I knew the car wasn't at mile twenty-two. When I hit the finish, I was still two miles from the car. Oh, man. Cars were parked on the side of the road, and I thought about asking someone for a ride. *They wouldn't kill me, right?* I assessed my supplies and I was prepared for the extra distance. I decided to do it on foot. I could have walked it, but running was quicker so I ran the final two. I was happy to get back, and I looked back at the valley, proud of what I'd run and the distance I'd covered—twenty-four miles instead of twenty-two. I had enjoyed seeing some new sights, revisiting some old ones, and genuinely having a great run. Sure, some of my body parts hurt, but this was the end of all the hard work: after tomorrow, my training was basically done. I felt accomplished, I felt strong, I felt like an ultra athlete.

For day two, I chose to do the McCullough Hills Trail close to my home. Yesterday, I wore the old Hokas, today I wore the new ones. I ran up and over the Amargosa section with ease, and by *ease*, I mean that I knew how to take it with respect and within my abilities. I walked the steep parts without worry about the time it was taking, I quick-stepped steep downhills, and fell into a pace for the flats. The new shoes felt good. I ran the full length of McCullough that by now I knew so very well. By the time I was returning home, I was filled with excitement. I just finished forty-six miles in two days. Forty-six miles! Was that good enough? It was three weeks until the fifty-miler. I engaged my mind-control. Trust the process.

Every difficult step that sounded impossible back in October—I had done it. I felt proud of myself. The work felt like money in the bank, and now I just had to cash it in at the race. For the next three weeks, I had maintenance runs to keep me in shape, and two long-ish runs, an eighteen-miler and a fourteen-miler. These distances didn't make me anxious at all. The hard work was done.

* * *

Excerpt from the Becoming Ultra Podcast
Season 2 Episode 23
Two weeks of mental training, the taper
March 18

Scott: Hey, welcome to Becoming Ultra, Scott Jones, I'm here with Ian and Janet today. Only a couple of weeks away from the American River 50, that Janet has been so diligently training for. For four, five months? How long has it been?

Ian: Almost six months.

Scott: Why don't you catch us up on the training, what's new?

Ian: Janet, you had your last long run today, how did the eighteen miles feel today?

Janet: It ended up being twenty. It felt pretty good, I started out feeling great about it, but quickly realized that, I am pretty sore, not sore, just tired from last week. I did twenty-two on Saturday and twenty-four on Sunday of last week. I'm just trying to get used to that idea that I feel good, but I still have recovery that is going on.

Ian: All the training is really in the bank now. Last weekend was a really big one, having two long runs, your two biggest back-to-back runs. You were covering almost the whole fifty miles over those two days. It makes doing it all in one day just a little more feasible. You had the thirty miles the week before that. So these are massive distances from even where we were two months ago. So your body is taking it in its stride. How do you feel as far as nerves at this stage?

Janet: I don't think that has settled in yet. After the back-to-backs last weekend, I first really got in to the race website as far as the race course and everything. I had everything else on my mind, and when that was released, the hard work is done, I started looking at the race website. I want to know things like how much nutrition do I want to carry, I know the course is pretty well stocked, so how much do I want to depend on them, I don't want to be spending all my time stopping at the aid stations. They have a chart that shows miles to the next aid station. I've been thinking about what I want my crew to have at about the halfway point. That's keeping the nerves at bay.

Ian: Like anything, if you feel well prepared, it takes a little of the nervousness out of it. These are exactly the things to be focusing on at the end, getting to know the course, getting to know where the aid stations are. I'll write it on my forearm, where the aid stations are and the distances between them. And if it's a really mountainous course, I'll often put on the elevations of the high and the low points as well.

Scott: In the next couple of weeks, because you are so fit right now, and running is going really smoothly, you're gonna crave bigger distances. So how do you trust the training, trust the taper?

Ian: I'd say the first thing is not to be tempted to throw in one extra hard session, or one extra long run. It's tempting to feel like you're under prepared. Your training has been exactly what it needs to be. The danger in doing more is that it won't make you fitter, just more tired or injured. You've got to trust that what you've done to this point is enough, you're not going to get any fitter than you are right now, and that is enough to do the race. If you did nothing between now and race day, you'd still be perfectly fit to do it.

Scott: Take the energies you've been putting into the longer runs, and put them into things that are still training, but just not what your focus has been on. Like getting enough sleep every night, staying hydrated, going light on your alcohol. Just the basic stuff, and put that energy into the things that are about recovery and keeping your body where it needs to be. Whether that's stress from work, don't plan any big projects, if that's up to you. Try to keep your work life and your personal life even keel for now. At this point, during the taper, mentally what can help going into it?

Ian: At this stage, thinking about what are you going to be going through, being prepared for the expected things that might go wrong, like tired legs, how are you going to deal with that, how are you going to keep your motivation up? And the unexpected as well. Ultras are very much about problem solving. It's about trying to manage all the things that can go wrong and heading them off before we get to that. And really, just finding all the motivators you can for those later stages of the race when it's going to be tough and when you know it's going to be the points where you're thinking to yourself, "Why am I doing this? Why is this important to me? Cause I could just stop now." All those negative thoughts that come in, be prepared for them, knowing they are going to happen, just having all the good answers for them, the reasons why this is important for you, the reasons why you're committed to this, and why it will mean so much to you. A few simple ones that are probably universal to everyone, is you've done all the work to get here. And certainly another one is, if you drop out because you choose to drop out, remind yourself how bad you'll feel afterwards.

Scott: Put down a handful of mantras that you can fall back on and keep those in your head over the next couple of weeks so that it becomes second nature to drop into a three or four word mantra or quote, or something that is going to trigger those thoughts as to why you are where you are.

Janet: That's a good thing to keep in mind, because I have never thought to quit a race, ever in my entire life, but I don't know what it's like to run twenty more miles than I've run previously. So I'm sure that's going to come up, so I need to mentally think about that over the next few weeks so that when I'm faced with that, that it doesn't becoming overwhelming to the point where I can't solve it with, just walk, or just eat something, there needs to be a mental reasoning why I keep going.

Scott: I'm really excited to see how Janet and Krystal do. Thank you, I appreciate it.

CHAPTER 37

In the last podcast, Scott and Ian discussed motivations for the ultra. In the past we'd talked about injuries, gear, nutrition, and fear of the long runs, but at this point, there wasn't much else to discuss on these topics. I progressed just like they'd told me I would. I'd have pain, but it'd be manageable. I'd have doubts, but they were only fears. Motivation was something that I put some thought into but still didn't have a strong answer. I'd run so many races in my life that I didn't need a reason to finish. If I said I would finish a race and I was trained for it, only a physical barrier would stop me.

So I had to wonder, would something new happen to me during this race that would require me to dig deeper? Maybe I should have some reason or mantra in mind—something to tell myself when it got tough. I joined this project because I wanted something to sink my teeth into and focus my attention and efforts on. I wanted an impressive project that I could look back on one day and be proud that I accomplished it. Being absorbed in a project that challenged all my limits felt right. Some people find that focus in their work, but I did not, so I had to seek it out in projects like this.

So what could be my mantra? Ian had been saying since the first time I spoke to him, "Your body can do more than you think it can." I had lived this statement over the past five months. Constantly, I was able to get my body to do things that my brain thought were impossible. When the going got tough at the end of the marathon, I repeated, "One foot in front of the other." That kept me going. Hopefully, I would remember these mantras.

When I arrived at my Tuesday group run, Mandi handed a flower to each of us. I took mine and sniffed it; it was fragrant and sweet. Mandi told us that these were for Ellen, a woman we passed every week at about the three-mile marker. In daily life, I often shared my world with various people I didn't know much about. I walked my dog at the same time every morning and ran into some of the same people doing their routine, but we never got to know anything else about each other. Ellen was one of these people. When we ran up this one hill, she was always walking down. We each waved and said hello as we passed, and she gave us a huge smile and a "Good morning." A few weeks ago, she wasn't there. I'd briefly thought about what might be wrong to take her out of her routine, but the thought passed. Mandi had found out that Ellen lost her husband, so her daily routine had changed. We carried these flowers in the hope that we would see her. We set out for our run, flowers in hand, and got to the point where she should be, and sure enough, she was back in her routine. We each handed her a flower. She cried, I cried, and others did, too. I like to think our message to her was "Kindness exists even in the midst of pain."

This was one of the incredible things I was a part of during my training, something I never would have experienced without it, and I was very thankful. I hoped these moments would give me something that far outlasts the Becoming Ultra project. When we finished the run, I still had heel pain, but I wouldn't have wanted to be anywhere else on this day.

CHAPTER 38

The day to head to Sacramento finally arrived. It was time to get there and see what would happen. I was tired of thinking about it and tired of explaining it to others. I wanted to start.

I felt stressed about coordinating it all. Even as I headed to Sacramento I wondered if it would all work out. I had done a lot of travel planning to coordinate when Dan and I arrived with the arrival of my brother Tom and my mother. My friend Julie who was going to pace part of the race, had decided not to come; with her injury, she doubted her ability to do the mileage. I had booked a hotel room and a rental car. I had planned the race, figuring out where my family could see me and what I would need. I don't like being the center of attention, and it was difficult to tell people what they had to do. I had also planned for the race itself—what food I would carry, what I would want in a drop bag, how fast to go out, and which shoes to wear. The first half of the course was pavement; the second was trail. I knew I would wear my new Hokas for the trail, but what about the pavement? Could I wear trail shoes on the pavement, or road shoes on the trail? Yes, I was still debating my shoe choice. How cold would it be in the morning and how much extra clothes would I want? The planning had been endless.

Dan and I arrived and got settled in at the hotel. We had a suite with a separate bedroom that we were going to share with my mother and brother. After a short time, I headed back to the airport to pick up Krystal. She got in my car and after sharing pleasantries, we discussed this task ahead.

"So, what was your longest run?" I asked.

"Thirty miles," Krystal replied.

"Yeah, mine, too. So what do you think? Twenty more is no problem?" I shakily asked. I was scared and intimidated. I awaited her confident response, like she was when we met for my first marathon.

"Yeah. I don't know." She stared out the window.

The fact that she was unsure of the feat ahead of us brought me new levels of anxiety. Even though we were trained, there's a big difference between our longest run of thirty miles and the fifty we planned to do in a few days. We discussed pacing and how to know what pace was right in the beginning. I was worried about how the crew would be managed. I didn't want to be a burden on my family, I knew that it would be a long day for them, too.

"I feel bad for my family; they are going to be sitting around bored all day just waiting for me. I'm going to tell them they don't have to be at every aid station," I told Krystal.

"Don't worry about them. They knew what this was about when they agreed to come here and support you. They'll figure it out." She smiled at me.

That made me feel better. The wheels of this whole thing were already in motion; I just had to let it play out.

When we got back to the hotel, Krystal and I went out for a short five-mile run to preview the course. Across the street from our hotel was the river and the trail that went along it. This was the first time I'd ever run with Krystal, and she was as fast as I thought she was. We kept up about a nine-minute pace, which was way too fast for me two days before my first ultra, but there was excitement in the air and anticipation of what was to come. Although I was anxious, I was happy, too. This was a huge feat I was undertaking, and I was proud of myself for getting this far. We saw several interesting trails that shot off the main trail; we tried a few of them, but then caution pulled us back to reality. Twisting an ankle on one of these would be so stupid. We retreated to the main trail.

We went back to the hotel and met up with Dan. Krystal, Dan and I went out to get a bite to eat and had fun getting to know each other. We made it an early night; our families and everyone from the Becoming Ultra project arrived the following day.

The next morning, airport runs occupied my time. I opened the windows and fresh, mild air breezed through the car. I took in a deep breath. This would be perfect weather for the race tomorrow.

I arrived back at the hotel with my family, and we sat in the living room area of our room and relaxed for a while. Then we had to get going to join everyone from the Becoming Ultra project for a lunch meet-up. Dan was still in the bedroom, which was odd, so I went in to check on him. When I walked in and saw him lying on the bed, I felt a sinking feeling in my gut.

"Are you OK?" I asked.

"No. I don't know what's wrong," he replied. That was an unwelcomed response.

I sat next to him and felt his forehead as we discussed his symptoms. His forehead felt fine, but he looked drained of energy.

"Stay here and get some rest, and I'll be back to check on you in a few hours," I said.

He needed to save up his energy for tomorrow, and no one needed to catch whatever he had. That would be disastrous for me or Krystal.

My mom, my brother Tom, and I drove to the restaurant, where we met up with Krystal; her fiancé, Russ; and her mom and dad, as well as Scott; his wife, Lauren, and their two kids; and Ian. Even though I had "met" Scott and Ian numerous times for the podcast tapings, this was our first in-person meeting.

We had some lunch and got to know each other. And, of course, we discussed the big elephant in the room: the race. Ian had decided to run it, and there was a good chance he'd win it.

Scott and Ian asked what I would tell myself to keep going when times got tough. I said that the only reasons I would ever quit were if I broke something that would risk a permanent injury, or if I physically could not make myself go forward. My mantra would be the same as it was in the marathon: "One foot in front of the other." Hopefully that would help in this race, too.

I had other concerns about the race.

"What pace should I go out at?" I asked.

Ian replied, "You should be able to do a nine-minute pace."

I had no response. I hoped that was a joke. I was much more comfortable with a ten-thirty- or eleven-minute pace. I was just tired of thinking and talking about this. I just wanted to get to the race and see what would happen.

Tom and I discussed which legs he would pace. Several weeks ago when Julie told me she wouldn't make it, I hated to admit it, but I was relieved. It was one less piece in this very stressful puzzle. Tom was planning to run a leg from miles twenty-four to thirty and another from forty-one to the end. That sounded like a good plan.

Krystal and I discussed Dan's illness.

"What caused it?" she inquired.

"I don't know," I replied.

I couldn't help but feel glad that it was Dan who was sick and not Krystal or myself. A sense of shame passed through me, that feeling when you know you've done something wrong. That was bad karma building up, but I didn't care.

We left the restaurant and got back to the hotel. I was hoping to find Dan in the living room and feeling better. He was still in bed.

"Feel any better?" I asked.

"No. I don't know what to do," he said. He described that he had an intense pain in his gut and feared it might be appendicitis. Being out of our insurance network always amplified the fear of what could be wrong; I really hoped it wasn't something that bad.

I got out our insurance card and started looking around the area for open clinics that took our insurance. Dan looked up symptoms on the Internet, hoping to prove it wasn't his appendix about to burst. I could tell he felt horrible that this was happening the day before my race. I didn't need this stress today, but it had to be taken care of and it helped to keep my mind occupied. I wanted Dan to feel better, and I didn't want him to miss the race either.

"I'm gonna call Tabu," he said. Tabu was a college friend who was now a doctor.

After getting off the phone, Dan was confident it wasn't his appendix. I let out a deep breath I hadn't realized I was holding. He stayed in bed the rest of the night, never requesting to go to a care center.

I wanted to spend some time showing Dan the race route and discussing how to get to all of the aid stations. He was going to do the majority of the navigating since Tom was running parts of the race and my seventy-five-year-old mom who still used paper maps probably wouldn't be much help with directions. Plus, Tom had just gotten his first smartphone; he surely wasn't proficient with the map app yet.

But Dan didn't feel well enough to get out of bed. I wasn't even sure he'd be on the course tomorrow. I let Krystal's words come to me: my family was here to see me through this, and they knew what this was about. I just had to let go and trust that they'd figure it out if Dan was too sick to be there.

I set out my race clothes for the following morning, said my good nights, and laid down. Tomorrow was finally the day. I was going to run this thing—fifty miles. Assuming I didn't wake up sick.

CHAPTER 39

When I woke up on the morning of my first ultra, the room was pitch black. My first thought was *Finally.* Finally, it was time to do this. Finally, I could see what it was like to run nearly two marathons, one right after another. *Finally.*

Before getting out of bed, I took in a deep breath and slowly let it out. I assessed my health and found that I felt great. Nervous, sure, but my throat didn't hurt and my stomach felt good. *I didn't catch what Dan had!* He was still asleep and so were my mom and Tom. I got up, gathered my things and went into the bathroom to get ready. I had a set routine by now. I applied a thick layer of sunscreen, put Band-Aids on my heels in a spot that sometimes rubbed, and then I put on my outfit: visor over a Buff, toesocks into my shoes. I'd decided to wear my new Hokas for the whole race. Hopefully the extra tread they had for trails wouldn't be a hindrance on the road. They had more cushion than my road shoes, I know I would appreciate that. I pinned my number in a spot I hoped wouldn't bug me later. Nothing new on race day. Except for one thing—my bra had been chafing me in one spot on my last few long runs, so I affixed a large Band-Aid there. It was just a Band-Aid; what harm could that do?

When I got out of the bathroom, everyone was up. I checked on Dan. "How are you feeling?"

"Good," he half-heartedly smiled. "Don't worry about me.

Do your thing." I had my doubts that he felt any better, but I couldn't do anything for him. I appreciated that he wasn't burdening me with the truth.

"Thanks." I kissed him. On the cheek, of course; I still didn't want to catch what he had.

Soon, it was time to leave. I'd brought my pink robe from the marathon and debated wearing it to the start line. Before the marathon, I felt more excited and in a fun mood, but I still feared this ultra distance. What would happen to me past twenty-six miles? Or thirty-six? Or forty-six? *Oh God. I have to stop thinking about it.* I tossed the robe back in my room.

I went down to the lobby and met up with Krystal and Scott. We got into Scott's car and headed for the start line. It was so cold that I was shivering. I instantly regretted leaving the robe behind.

I had to use the bathroom, so I got in line. The air was damp and crisp. The pre-dawn twilight was just beginning to ease the darkness of night. I stood next to a lake that was probably a reservoir of the American River and saw moisture hovering just above the surface. I could hear the morning stillness and the gentle laps of tiny waves, as if I had super sensitive hearing. I let those sounds drown out the noise of the race starting area.

I finished up and got back to the car holding and rubbing my arms. Krystal's mom gave me a sweatshirt to wear. She was a sweetheart. There was still time to waste, so I got into Scott's car and Ian joined us. I didn't know what to say at this point. I couldn't make small talk with my mind preoccupied with the race, but I tried, "So how long do you think this will take me."

Scott replied, "Don't worry. You've got all day."

I took a sip from my hydration pack and got a mix of water and air. *Oh no! I knew I should have gotten a new one.* "Ugh, I don't think this is working right."

"Maybe the connection's loose," Scott offered.

It was time for Ian's group to start, so we all got out. I laid my pack on the ground and took the whole bladder apparatus out. There was *no* way I could run this without my hydration pack. I checked the hose at the bottom, and sure enough, it wasn't pushed in all the way. How stupid. It was something I'd done so many times before; how could I screw it up today? I got it put in right and took a sip of just water this time. Crisis one averted.

Ian's group took off; mine and Krystal's would leave shortly. Krystal and I met up with Alison; I tried to find Beth, who I'd run with at Cowboy Trails during my training, but could not. We took selfies, shared frightened glances—at least that's what mine were—and wished each other well.

Then we were off. To run fifty miles. Just like that. I let the pack of runners settle in around me and started on a nice, very slow-feeling pace. The sky was in full twilight now, so the morning felt young and fresh. There was no race feel to this start; no one was maneuvering for position. Everyone understood that this was an endurance challenge that would take all day. I took in a deep breath and looked around as the trees sparkled with dew and runners rhythmically moved among them. Before I knew it, I no longer had fifty miles to run; there were only forty-nine left.

For about the first eight miles, we ran along the lake and then we did an out and back down the river for about seven miles each way. During this time, I enjoyed the start to a beautiful day. The sun warmed me up and the trees along the path provided shade. I came upon Beth around mile eight. We ran together for a short while, and then drifted apart. I saw this couple on the side of the trail, sitting in lawn chairs with a large portable radio playing zydeco tunes. I waved at them and thanked them for being there.

The course was paved during this section and we shared the path with bicyclists. They weren't happy we were there and many of them commented that we were on the wrong side of the path. The signs along the path told us to be on one side, and the bikers yelled that we should be on the other side. I decided to ignore their comments and keep the negativity out of my brain; I didn't need that right now.

I was receiving texts from friends and family asking about my progress, and I was texting back about how far along I was and how good I felt. I ran with a small group of people for several miles; we exchanged names and small talk. I chatted with a guy struggling up a hill on long rollerblades that looked like skis. He said a year ago he couldn't walk. He said us runners were inspiring to him. I told him that he was the inspiration.

I cruised through the Negro Bar aid station at mile twenty. It was the first station that allowed spectators, and Dan, my mom, and Tom were there. They cheered me in. I slammed down a Rice Krispy treat and bragged about how I could eat whatever I wanted. It was uplifting to see my family. I solo run races so often that I didn't think this would matter, but it did; it meant a lot. They likely spent a lot of time waiting to see me for just a few seconds, and then I was off.

Miles twenty through twenty-four remained fun. I joined the small group again, and we chatted some more. We again ran by the lawn-chair-and-radio couple still playing zydeco songs, but in a whole new location. They were sitting there, relaxed and settled as if they'd been in this place all day. I high-fived them and thanked them again for being there.

So far, this ultra was a breeze. I felt strong and full of energy, but I felt reserved in my pace, confident that I could keep this up for the distance. I got into a groove of eating a food item —a waffle cookie, peanut butter and jelly sandwich, or my sweet potato mix—on the hour, and a sugar item like cranberries or gummy energy chews on the half hour. Just like in training.

Beal's Point aid station at mile twenty-four was coming up quickly. I assessed my situation and planned for the stop. I felt fine, and my food supply was fine. I wanted to reapply sunscreen and check the Band-Aids on my heels. Other than that, I planned to make this a quick stop and be on my way.

When I ran into Beal's Point, the atmosphere was like a finish line. There were a lot of people there with all the supplies you could ever need, as well as the bag drop. My family had brought mine, so I didn't have to search for it. I emptied the contents out on the ground. I grabbed the sunscreen and applied it liberally all over. I sat down and took my shoes off to check my Band-Aids; they were still in place. I grabbed a few more waffle cookies from my bag, and then shoved everything back in. I overdid it with the sunscreen and had to spend extra time rubbing in the thick white film.

"Your running is very upright," my mom noted.

"That's the physical therapy at work," I replied. My mom had watched me run in a lot of races, so she should know my gait. It was good to hear that it was visibly different and better.

Dan gave me a kiss, this time on the lips. If I caught what he had, it wouldn't kick in for a few days.

"Are you feeling better?" I asked.

"I'm fine," he replied.

I said my thank yous and was off again. This time, Tom ran with me. "I hope you're prepared to run slow," I said.

"Whatever you can do. You set the pace," he replied.

My pace was about ten-thirty- to eleven-minutes up to this point. The pain was starting in my knees, but it wasn't too bad and my steps were still solid. The midmorning sunshine was heating up the day, but the shady spots through the woods tempered that. Tom and I got to talking about his wife and kids. Our families live far away from each other and I'm not good on the phone, so we weren't close. It was good to hear him talk of raising his children. He'd just been through a renovation of his house so we talked about that, too.

I saw the group again and I introduced my brother. Our paces differed, however, and they drifted away again.

"Minimal versus maximal," I heard a runner say to us.

I turned and the guy was pointing at my feet. Tom was wearing toe shoes, and I was wearing the thickest soles running shoes made.

"Haha. I'll let you know which does better," I replied. My legs hurt despite all this cushioning. I couldn't imagine wearing minimalist shoes right now.

Tom told me that he'd been wearing those toe shoes for

years. I asked about the barefoot craze, and he explained how it can help posture and hence relieve all types of pain. I told him of my physical therapy experience and how I'd not associated inexplicable pains with muscle strength before.

I don't know how much pacing was done during these miles. He just followed my pace and kept me company. We saw the radio couple again, sitting in a new spot, but just like before, they looked like they'd been in this spot all day. I told Tom how I'd been seeing them all along the course. I waved to them and thanked them again, but I didn't run over to them this time. That would take me a few steps off course and at this point, I didn't feel like making this feat any longer.

"Do you want me to take some pictures? Or wait till the later leg?" Tom asked.

Arguably, the second leg he was pacing was going to be more picturesque, but the course wasn't crowded here. "We better just do it now."

He ran ahead in a few spots and took pictures and video of me running. We had fun running and chatting through the woods and fields; I felt like we were kids again. We approached the Granite Bay aid station at the thirty-mile mark. My body felt spent and pain was a throbbing constant, but I still felt strong. Past thirty miles was the great unknown. The same question I'd asked myself countless times returned: *How the heck am I going to run twenty more miles?*

CHAPTER 40

When we got to Granite Bay, Dan and my mom were waiting. Tom stopped and stayed with them. He probably could have run the rest of it with me, but that didn't happen, and that was fine with me. I knew there was work to do here, and it started now. I wanted to spend some of that time figuring it out on my own. My pace had slowed down to about twelve-thirty, and this next part was going to be tough: exposed trail along the river and a long eight miles before the next aid station. I topped off my water, and then I was off into the unknown.

As I ran, I assessed my aches and pains. My legs were fatigued, and my joints, especially my knees, were sore, but I had no sharp pain. My feet were landing solidly; they were supporting me on this terrain. The Band-Aids I'd put under my bra were irritating me, so they were probably not preventing the chaffing, but I wasn't going to do anything about it right now. Ian's words came to me: "Your body can do more than you think it can." I still had a really long way to go. I had to stop focusing on the pain, be grateful that I was able to keep moving. I relied on my training and the experience of Ian and Scott, who said that my body was prepared for this. I could still move forward. One foot in front of the other.

I kept going. At mile thirty-three, my stomach started to feel queasy. The terrain was really tough: lots of ups and downs in the trail with boulders that I needed to climb over and stairs in the trail. It seems like it might be a fun hiking trail—if I wasn't thirty-three miles into a fifty-mile race. This section was also gorgeous. I was high above the river on a bluff covered with flowers and large wild grass fields. Vistas opened up exposing coves and large lake-like areas. The views reminded me of camping at Devil's Lake in Wisconsin when I was a kid and hiking trails that wound around rock formations high above the lake. I tried to let my mind stay in the past for a while, but the heat brought me back. The trail was exposed to the sun and the promising day I'd been enjoying earlier had turned into a hot afternoon. It was eighty-two degrees around noon, not unlike the desert conditions I was used to, but my body was spent.

This section was tougher than I expected and tougher than anything I'd ever done. I needed energy. On most long runs, taking in sugar gave me a kick, but sugar wasn't doing it anymore, and that was all the food I had. I texted my family to have my bag available at mile forty. The sports drink I was drinking had both salt and sugar; I needed just salt. Up until now, I was doing what I'd always done, but what worked in training for thirty miles—and for the first thirty miles today—wasn't working anymore.

I was passing a section of shorter grass when I heard a rattle. I continued putting one foot in front of the other along the path, and when I turned my head, I saw a rattlesnake curled up. I ran past it and kept going. A bit delayed I realized, *That was a rattlesnake! I could have been bit. I could have taken a picture of it.* I could tell I was losing brain power. When I heard people say that anything can happen in an ultra, I wasn't expecting rattlesnakes. I felt lucky to have passed it without incident.

I was getting closer to the Horseshoe Bar aid station at mile thirty-eight. I saw a girl with no water system and she was asking runners for water to spare. *Who the heck comes on this stretch after all these miles without water?* I felt my pack and there wasn't much to spare. Plus, my stomach was getting worse. I wondered if I should give her some water. I spent a lot of time contemplating on this, and someone else gave her some water before I'd decided. Great, more bad karma.

I got to Horseshoe Bar, and it was like a heavenly retreat. I got some boiled, salted potatoes but they were tough to get down. I went to the bathroom, which was a welcome relief. I hoped that would solve my stomach problems. They also had a bucket of ice water, and I dunked my Buff in it. Putting it back on my head was the best moment of my entire life. I felt refreshed; I felt human again. Only twelve miles left of this run. I'd run that distance so many times over the last six months. *Just twelve more miles.*

After three more miles, I approached Rattlesnake Bar aid station. The cooling effect of the ice water had worn off quickly, and the bathroom stop wasn't what I needed. I could hear a crowd at the aid station, but I couldn't get there, not yet. Something had to give. I leaned off to the side of the trail and puked. I stayed bent over, allowing myself a moment. I knew my family was waiting at the next aid station. I knew I still had nine miles to go. There was absolutely no way this ended here, but I wondered how I was going to run nine more miles. "You've got all day," Scott had said. I took a deep breath, stood up, and kept running.

I ran into the Rattlesnake Bar aid station at mile forty-one and found my family.

"You're looking good," my mom said.

I glanced in her direction, running my tongue along my teeth. Could I just keep it a secret? I decided, even though it was gross and embarrassing, that I ought to let them know the condition I was in. "I just puked up there, right before I came down here."

They all gave me a sad look, but thankfully no one pressed me to stop. For one second, my brain offered the idea to quit. Not so much as a true possibility, but more as a smart-side-of-the-brain option to consider. No one would blame me. I thought about my family and how long they'd already been sitting around waiting for me and how long it would take me to finish this thing. I also thought about all the training I'd done, all the early mornings, the twenty-plus-milers; I thought about the forty-one miles I'd already run. If I quit now, I'd have to do all this again on another day. And with that thought, the idea went away; there was absolutely no way I was going to quit at this point. I didn't have a predetermined allowable reason to quit. Nothing was irreversibly damaged, and I could physically make myself go forward. So, on it was.

My mom handed me the bag I requested. I looked through it for supplies, but nothing looked good. I walked to the aid station and forced down more potatoes and chips. I walked back to my family. I hunched up my shoulders, lowered my head and said, "Let's get it done." Tom rejoined me and we set off.

My pace had slowed from thirteen to seventeen minutes during the thirty-to-forty-one-mile segment, and now I was going even slower. There was no longer any texting; my brain couldn't manage it. These were slow, tough miles. I puked a few more miles in, and then had a burst of energy. One foot in front of the other. I ran for a while—a half mile? A quarter? Who knows. I looked around at the beautiful scenery, and the sun was starting to wane in the sky. A day full of promise was now heading to completion. We had moved away from the river and were in among the trees. I thought that the pictures Tom had taken of me earlier would look better here, but I was in no condition to deal with that. I was glad we had done that in the earlier segment.

We got to Dowdin's Post aid station at mile forty-four. Tom went to talk to the volunteers to see if they had any kind of pill for my problems. They didn't. I wasn't sure I wanted to add anything new to the mix anyway. All I wanted at this point was my bed. I wanted to curl up and give my leg muscles and joints a break. I wanted to stop jostling my stomach. I wanted to let my brain relax. I couldn't. I shoved these thoughts aside. I was so close. There was no stopping.

Soon after we got moving again, I heaved into the bushes. As I stood there, Tom tried to comfort me with his hand on my back, but he was standing downwind. I swung my arm at him so he wouldn't get any of my mess on him. I hoped he didn't think I was swatting his hand away, but I didn't have the energy to explain myself. My brain could only handle the one task of keeping my body together. After vomiting, I had a burst of energy and was able to run for a while. One foot in front of the other.

I worried about the puking. It meant a lot of things I couldn't deal with right now: dehydration, lightheadedness, and loss of energy. I needed to take in calories to fuel myself, so I couldn't keep puking them up. From training, I knew that sugar would give me a burst of energy, so I was worried about being able to finish this race without it. I went to get a snack from my pack, remembered it was a sugar gummy, and decided against it. Two seconds later I wanted it again, and then decided against it. This went on for some time. I was like a computer stuck in a loop, unable to stop from repeating and having no power button to hit Restart.

I still had a long way to go, but there wasn't anything I could do about getting energy. Ian's words rang in my head—"A lot can go wrong." It sounded simple enough when I had thought about this before the race. Now that I knew my issue was an upset stomach, it was tremendously difficult to cope with. I fell back on my mantra, one foot in front of the other. That was something I could still do.

I stopped looking at my watch in this stretch, and later I learned the battery died around mile forty-seven. I was concerned about the cutoff, the time the race officials gave you to complete the course. I wasn't sure when it was, or how close I was to it. Truthfully, I couldn't do anything about it even if I was close, I was incapable of speeding up at that point. Again, I thought about Scott's words: "You've got all day." It looked like I was going to need it. I was going to finish when I could, whether there was a finish line waiting for me or not.

A fellow runner offered me a tube of salt. Tom took it. I obviously screwed up my salt intake because the straight salt tasted so good. Tom helped immensely with this, as he took instructions from the guy who gave it to us. My brain just could not manage remembering what he'd said. All I could control was moving forward. Tom would give me the tube, and I'd take a pinch and give it back. We repeated that process for a while. He said take more, and I did it. I didn't talk about it, I didn't question it, I just did what he said. I felt better, but there was no climbing out of this hole.

CHAPTER 41

I finally got to the appropriately named Last Gasp aid station. Forty-seven miles done. Scott was there waiting for me; he had been here since Krystal passed through, which was probably several hours ago. Tom went to talk to him to tell him my condition, no doubt. I shuffled over to the aid tent hoping something looked good. I leaned on a pole of the tent to look over the table of supplies. I wanted a Coke, I could see it there on the table, but other runners kept coming into the aid tent and cutting me off. I stood, supporting myself on the post, unable to take the steps to get to the Coke. I tried several times to get there and failed. It was pretty sad. Scott went and got one and handed it to me. I let out a sigh of relief and tried to smile at him. Thoughts of lying down overpowered everything; I let go of the post and took my Coke to a grassy gravel spot at the edge of the parking lot.

"You shouldn't sit," Scott said. He sounded distant and not at all convincing. I collapsed and sat on the grassy stones. If I didn't lie down, that was at least something.

I could feel my stomach revolting. I twisted and turned away from Scott and Tom, supporting myself on my arms and heaved up yet again. My head hung low.

I should have been discouraged and crying, but I wasn't. I was tired of the puking, that's for sure, but this was just my story. This was the culmination of everything I'd put into this, and the finish line was where this would end, not here. I wasn't upset; as Ian said, anything can go wrong. I was thankful that this was something I could still move forward with.

I pushed myself up from the ground, and Tom helped get me to my feet.

I drank the Coke and had some potato chips. The final three miles were going to take a long time, and I needed water for it. Tom took my hydration pack and filled the reservoir. My pace had slowed to nearly twenty minutes. Could that even be considered running? I wondered if Tom realized he was coming out here for such a long walk. The next three miles were up a hill, a really big hill that would take me nearly one thousand feet in elevation gain. I rolled my eyes, donned my pack, and got ready to head out.

"Are you going to make it to the end?" Scott was filming my answer for a video he was planning on making for the Becoming Ultra website.

I stared at him for a moment, and then answered honestly, "I don't know."

He put the camera down and said, "Wrong answer."

We laughed, sort of. It wasn't that I was going to quit mentally; it really wasn't. I just wasn't sure if my body would physically make it. I was so close, it seemed impossible not to make it at this point, but I had visions of runners whose legs turned to Jell-O and just couldn't function. I hoped that wouldn't happen to me, but I still had three challenging miles left.

We got started. Tom and Scott accompanied me for the final miles. It was the perfect distraction. Conversation topics were random; following trains of thought that didn't stick, but the time passed. I noticed Tom's hydration pack was just a regular backpack that he retrofitted. He talked about how he'd done it; he was always a creative innovator like that. Then we skipped to another topic. I told Scott I was writing a memoir about my Becoming Ultra experience. We talked about other books I'd written, namely, one in the sci-fi genre. He asked what kind of sci-fi authors I liked, and I laughed because I couldn't think of a single one I'd ever read. Scott talked about his wife and raising his kids and getting to run a business from home. We continued the climb up this humongous hill.

The hill should have been hell, but it was actually welcome. No one around us was running, so there was no pressure to do anything but put one foot in front of the other. Fortunately, it seemed my body was physically prepared for this. I had pain, absolutely, but not sharp, agonizing pain; just the dull, constant pain of trying to use muscles that were completely spent.

My dreams of lying down continued. There was a wooden fence along part of the course, the kind made up of posts supporting two horizontal logs. I veered off, stopped, and leaned against it. Scott and Tom both warned against this. I didn't stay long. I just needed to feel the action of stopping. I looked around and saw the sun getting close to setting. A day I'd seen start fresh was now getting ready to end, and I got to experience the whole thing. I was alive today. I felt the effort of expending myself past all my boundaries, and it was deeply humanizing. I pushed away from the fence post onto legs that screeched at me and a stomach that turned. I stopped just that one time, because starting again was horribly difficult.

Over an hour after leaving Last Gasp, I heard noises of a crowd. It was a heavenly sound, and my spirits instantly lifted. I turned a corner and saw the shoot funneling me to the finish. People were gathered all along the way, and I started to run. I ran past everyone as they cheered, waving to all of them and grateful for the encouragement. I crossed the finish line with a huge smile on my face. Fifty miles in one day—done!

CHAPTER 42

After I crossed the finish line, I was handed a finisher's medal and a Patagonia sweatshirt with an embroidered American River 50 logo. I took my loot and saw a beautiful patch of grass not too far from where I was. It wasn't exactly my bed, but all I'd been thinking about was lying down, and it looked good enough. I made a beeline for it, but Scott stepped in my path.

"Janet, let me ask you some questions," he raised his camera to film what I had to say.

Seriously dude, fuck you. Get out of my way.

Fortunately, something much more polite actually came out of my mouth, "I'm so mad at you right now."

I don't remember the interview, I'm sure he wanted to know if I was proud of myself. I was. If I was in pain. I was. If I would do this again. I'd need some time for that question. I wasn't in tears, I didn't feel overwhelmed by my accomplishment, at least not there in the finish area. I did feel immense relief that it was done. I was glad to be able to stop moving so that hopefully my stomach would calm down. I also felt at a loss. For six months, after every longest distance ever I had run, there was another accomplishment waiting for me on my schedule. But this was it. There was nothing else left to do or think about.

When Scott lowered the camera, Dan, Tom, and my mom were there. They all hugged me and gave me praises. My need to lay down subsided long enough to let them lead me to the area they had been waiting for me. Krystal, her family, Scott, and Ian were all there, too. I plopped down in an empty chair and put my head in my hands letting the weight of everything rest for a while. Everyone was offering to get me whatever I needed, but I just wanted to get to my bed and lay down. Krystal said they were offering massages in the finish area, but I declined. The thought of someone touching me right now conjured up images of me violently attacking such an aggressor.

As we sat and I gathered the strength to make it to the parking lot, I learned that Dan had been sick all day. Regardless, he struggled through and was there at every aid station and helped my mom out. She's fairly spry for a seventy-five-year-old, but she's still seventy-five and needs help. I felt bad for him but was proud that he'd been there for me and my mom. I also learned that Krystal's family had helped my mom out, too, in maneuvering some of the aid stations. I thanked them. I couldn't believe they stuck around and waited for me to finish; that was cool. I learned that Krystal had won the Spirit Award for the race, an award that the race officials gave to someone who embodied the spirit of the race. She carried the American flag the last three miles of the race, from Last Gasp aid station to the end. In her races, she often carried it. I could not have managed that, but I'm glad she got to do it and that the race officials recognized her for it. I also learned that Ian had finished third overall, in six hours and seventeen minutes. Jesus. I was out there almost twice as long!

We didn't spend much time there after I arrived, and soon we began our way back to the hotel. I wanted to be transported there, like, by teleportation. Unfortunately, that technology does not exist. The hotel was about twenty-five miles back the way I'd just run, and it sounded exhausting to get there even by car. I had difficulty walking to the car, which was weird because I just ran fifty miles. How could this extra one hundred feet be such a problem? Dan started driving and within ten minutes, my stomach started to revolt again. I was able to get out,

"Plastic bag!" My mom frantically looked for something as Dan pulled off the road. I let out one more batch from my stomach.

Once we were back in the room, I finally got to curl up in bed. It felt every bit as amazing as I thought it would. When I finished the race, I didn't initially feel the pride I thought I would. I was in pain and just wanted to feel better. I thought I'd want to eat tons of food afterward, but all I had was a cup of soup.

The next morning I woke up feeling pretty good. I squatted down to the floor without any joint pain and just a little hip pain. When I got in the shower, I realized that the pain from my bra was actually a raw spot outlining the Band-Aid I had put in place to prevent that. Nothing new on race day. But that was the only raw skin I had, so I was OK with it. We had an easy day planned and went to a tourist area in downtown Sacramento. I got wiped out pretty easily, and we retreated back to the hotel.

That night I didn't sleep well. I was in the bathroom at least fifteen times. Awfulness was escaping from the other end. After each time, I went to the kitchen and ate a pinch of salt. My guess is that I screwed up my stomach from trying to drink all my salt instead of taking straight salt or salt tablets. I don't know whether I caught Dan's sickness, but at that point, it didn't really make a difference. My body just needed time to recover.

Before leaving California, we visited San Francisco and Alcatraz, a place that was on my bucket list. I had a great time with my family and was so thankful that they'd come out to do this with me and that we got to spend some time together.

During the boat trip from the dock to Alcatraz, I looked out on the bay and reflected on the feat I'd completed. I did something that seemed so impossible just a short time ago; that was impressive. I called upon my muscles, and they answered. That wasn't willpower, luck, or anything mystical—that was training. The hard work and commitment I'd put to this over the past six months was there for me when I needed it. I ran 1,012 miles over six months, with 69,110 feet of total elevation gain—that's more than two Mount Everests! Although I thought

I was trained with the ability to complete the fifty miles in about ten hours, it took me eleven hours and fifty minutes. Because things go wrong in ultras, and things definitely went wrong for me. Regardless, I'm glad I took this on. I'm glad I didn't wait for "one day" to do something like this.

* * *

Excerpt from the Becoming Ultra Podcast Season 2 Episode 25
Janet's first fifty-miler. A recap
April 14

Scott: Hey, welcome to Becoming Ultra, I'm Scott Jones your host. And this is the fun stuff right here. Janet Patkowa has been training for an amazing feat of fifty miles for six months with her coach, Ian Sharman. A week and a half ago, it all came to a head, she got to go out there and compete at the American River 50. Today we're going to do a follow up. Ian, why don't you ask some post questions of Janet.

Ian: Now that you've had some time to think about it, how would you describe the race, the positives and negatives?

Janet: First of all, one through thirty was amazing. It was the greatest experience ever. I controlled my pacing exactly how I wanted to, I didn't feel like I went out too fast. The miles went by easily, I was chatting with people, taking in the scenery and everything. Then it got tough, after the part that I knew. Oh, and the nutrition and salt went great for miles one through thirty. After thirty, my muscles were starting to feel like it was quite a challenge, but I remembered you saying that your body can do more than you think it can, so I just said, nothing's breaking, I'm putting my feet down with solid steps. I'm not going to worry about the pain right now, I'm just going to move forward. But then, my stomach got a little upset and queasy, and around mile forty, I threw up, and eventually ended up throwing up four times in the race. Which was not great, but I just kept it in my head that I'd done six months of training, I'd already done forty miles of this race, if I can make myself go forward, then I am going forward. So, I worried more about my muscles seizing up or fainting. My brother was running with me for the end part.

So it was really helpful because he was able to better monitor me than I was able to do, he would say, here take some salt, and I'd do it. That's what I think I screwed up was I didn't take in enough salt early enough, there was a stretch from about thirty-three to forty that was really exposed, there was no aid station in there, and I think I just got that part screwed up. It didn't break my resolve, I was completely committed to finishing it, as long as I could get there. It wasn't the greatest part of the experience, but I just wanted to finish it. So, I was really proud of myself when I got across that finish line.

Ian: The fact that you can say the first thirty miles were great, wasn't very difficult, you were totally on top of things, that's thirty miles. That's an ultra in itself. The stomach problems that you had, very common in ultras, and it doesn't mean your race is over. The fact that you were able to mentally deal with it, that's the big thing. You knew physically you could keep moving, and as long as you kept that certainty in there, you did. If you'd have allowed the negative thoughts to creep in, like oh no, I'm having a dodgy stomach now, how am I going to keep going, my race is over, I'm now slowed right down. It's so easy to become negative, it wasn't fun, but you were able to keep yourself positive enough, and motivated enough to keep moving, and really that's what ultras are all about. You can do more than you think, and it's largely up to your mind.

Scott: I went down to the last aid station to interview Janet. She came into the aid station, and grabbed the canopy, and she just wanted Coke. She couldn't take another step to get it, like four people cut in front of her, so I just went through everybody and grabbed her some. Then she goes to collapse, and we get her to sit down. Then it all just came up. I don't want to say she came back from the dead, but she was in a really tough place, physically, for a runner. It was really inspiring. To see her get up, choke down some potato chips, get some salt in her system, and start hiking the last three miles up that hill, it was really, really cool. So Janet, that was an awesome moment.

Ian: It's how you cope with things that make it interesting and rewarding. It's what the human spirit is all about. We can push ourselves so much harder than we think we can.

Scott: What's the one big takeaway that you learned about

yourself?

Janet: I learned so much. I think what it would be is if I pick a goal, I know I can do it. I think that this can mean so much for many different things in my life, not even having to do with running. I know that if I pick a goal, and I set myself to it, I can get there. The steps maybe have to be small, maybe I need help along the way, but I can get there, if I just keep my eye on what I want.

Scott: What is next for you as a runner?

Janet: Well, that is the question, I guess. Would I do something like this again? I can say I wouldn't be intimidated to pick out a race like this. If it was fifty miles or less, I'd say yeah, sure, no problem. But I definitely respect the fifty-mile distance now, I would not jump into a fifty-miler unless I knew I had the time to prep for it.

Scott: Janet, thank you so much. Listeners, thank you so much. Thank you guys so much for listening. Wrap up with Janet Patkowa, who is now awesomely an ultra runner.

CHAPTER 43

Within a month, I was back to normal, mostly. I didn't eat sugar for two days after the ultra, which is extremely rare for me. My gut took a good three days to get better, and still another few after that to be back to 100 percent. I didn't care; it would get back to normal eventually and I was patient.

I didn't run again until a week after the ultra. I respected the fifty miles, and I respected the recovery that was required and let it happen. My two pinky toenails were black after the race and the nails fell off after a month or so, but they grew back. A space had appeared under the big toenail of my right foot, but that grew out after about six months. My heel didn't feel better, and I went to see a physical therapist. Turns out I had plantar fasciitis, and over the following year I learned more about my feet than I ever cared to. I'm still coping with that condition, but I'm able to run, just not as much, which is fine with me.

The overwhelming moment of pride I was expecting didn't happen at the finish line. Instead, it happened at three separate times. The first occurred when I finished the final back-to-back, my twenty-four- and twenty-two-milers. That was the end of all the work and the moment when I got to see just how much effort was required to get trained for the ultra. The second occurred when I was driving a few weeks after the race, windows open and my hair was blowing in the wind, singing along to a song on the radio like I was sixteen again and driving in a car alone for the first time. I saw the mountain with the Amargosa trail rising from the road, and I felt free. I was so proud that I could go run that now without even thinking about it. The third time was when I was going to my Thursday morning Run Grrrls Run group. These girls, and my Tuesday group, helped me accomplish the ultra. Without them, I would either have had to run all those miles alone, on a treadmill, or I just wouldn't have run them. I was humbled that I got to be a part of those groups. Maybe having pride of accomplishing something isn't about the accomplishment itself, but the journey that gets you there.

I was also thankful to my brother Tom who took the time away from his family to pace me. I don't know if I would have gotten to the end without him. The help of others is required to accomplish feats like this, or to at least make the journey more fun. I was thankful for Dan, who encouraged me even though this was time-consuming and took up many weekends. I was thankful my mom got to come out and see me race, just like she had when I was a kid.

I wouldn't have done any of this if it wasn't for Scott. I was thankful that he'd picked me, had faith in me to finish it, and encouraged me throughout the training. I was thankful for Ian as well, for his expertise and patience, and getting me to the end without an injury.

I didn't plan to train like that forever, so I thought about the parts of the training that I liked and didn't like. I liked getting to be out on the trails for hours. I liked the peace and solitude and enjoyed being alone. I liked expending my energy and feeling content because of it. I enjoyed the energy of race day and getting to see new trail while having aid stations there for support. On the other hand, I didn't like the time consumption of the back-to-back runs. Not only were the runs long, but I was spent for the rest of the day. I didn't want running to become my life, but I wanted it to be a part of it. I saw value in the fitness it brought me. I spent the next year not taking on any serious running goals. I had to get a handle on the plantar fasciitis so that I didn't do any permanent damage.

I learned that if I dream about doing something, I should actually take the steps to get there. I learned that a large project is just a succession of smaller, more manageable steps. I can't sit around waiting for "one day" to do all the things I want to do only to find that one day never arrives. One day is not a thing waiting in the cosmos to grace me with its presence. One day happens when I make it happen. I discovered that I am the adventurous person I wanted to be, and that big adventures can fit into my life right now. Maybe having big dreams isn't about creating an all new path in life, but instead pushing the boundaries of the things I already enjoyed. I need to revisit some of my dreams for retirement and see what I can start working on today. Maybe I need to find a mountain to climb, or start looking for a backpacking trek. What other adventures can I accomplish if I just decide to get started?

Made in the USA
Middletown, DE
07 September 2020

19007044R00118